BUGLES IN THE AFTERNOON

Smyth & Helwys Publishing, Inc.
6316 Peake Road
Macon, Georgia 31210-3960
1-800-747-3016
©2016 by Judson Edwards
All rights reserved.

All Scripture references are from the *Common English Bible* (copyright 2011).

Library of Congress Cataloging-in-Publication Data

Names: Edwards, Judson, author.
Title: Bugles in the afternoon : dealing with discouragement and
    disillusionment in ministry / by Judson Edwards.
Description: Macon : Smyth & Helwys, 2016.
Identifiers: LCCN 2016000029 | ISBN 9781573128650 (pbk. : alk. paper)
Subjects: LCSH: Clergy--Psychology. | Clergy--Religious life. | Clergy--Job
    stress.
Classification: LCC BV4398 .E39 2016 | DDC 253/.2--dc23
LC record available at http://lccn.loc.gov/2016000029

Advance Praise for *Bugles in the Afternoon*

Books on ministry usually lie. They describe only the trumpets in the morning or the cello at the end of the day. Judson Edwards helps us hear the Bugles in the Afternoon. He tells the truth about how difficult and delightful it is to serve Christ's church. I am grateful for such an honest book on ministry,

—Brett Younger
McAfee School of Theology
Atlanta, Georgia

With *Bugles in the Afternoon*, Jud Edwards will bless and enlighten. His unflinching, poignant examination of ministry will help pastors and congregational staff realize they are not alone and, despite momentary appearances to the contrary, they can not only endure, but thrive. Likewise, his transparent, honest reflection on ministry will help lay leaders understand and support the clergy they have called to lead them.

—Marv Knox
Editor, Baptist Standard
Plano, Texas

Jud Edwards writes honestly, creatively, and thoughtfully about being a pastor. He's realistic but never cynical. He offers clear guidance but never simplistic formulas. He acknowledges that ministry can be hard, but affirms that it also a source of joy.

—Guy Sayles
Mars Hill University
Mars Hill, North Carolina

BUGLES IN
THE AFTERNOON

Dealing with Discouragement
and Disillusionment in Ministry

JUDSON EDWARDS

Also by Judson Edwards

A Matter of Choice
Running the Race
Dancing to Zion
The Coffee Pot Letters
The Case of the Uptight Christian
Relationship Therapy
The Leadership Labyrinth
Hidden Treasures
Making the Good News Good Again
Blissful Affliction
Quiet Faith

In Memory of Glen Edwards,
good company under the juniper tree

CONTENTS

INTRODUCTION

When I began my work as a pastor more than forty years ago, I bought a book titled *Trumpets in the Morning*. The book was written by a well-known pastor who celebrated the fact that he got to hear trumpets every morning, summoning him to serve the Lord and make an eternal difference in the world. I wanted that book in my library because that is exactly what I wanted for myself and my ministry. I, too, wanted to hear trumpets in the morning and rise up every day to serve the Lord and make an eternal difference in the world.

It was, as I recall, a fine book and one I dipped into often, especially when discouragement and disillusionment came calling. And, much to my surprise, they *did* come calling. In fact, I sometimes became so discouraged and disillusioned that I couldn't hear those trumpets at all.

I began my work as a pastor filled with youthful idealism and fully expecting to become a ministerial star. I was going to preach spellbinding sermons, impress people with my keen insight and deep theology, and not so gradually climb the ladder of ecclesiastical success. In short, I was going to hear those trumpets every morning and respond with a faith and vigor that would land me in a prestigious pulpit in no time at all.

But while I was in seminary, I found myself pastoring a church so far out in the country that the trumpets could barely be heard. Sherry and I made a 350-mile round trip every weekend to be with those loving people in central Texas, and, for our efforts, we made a whopping fifty dollars a week. On a "big Sunday," we had forty people in worship, and I got ecstatic if we ever topped fifty. But this was just my seminary church, and I knew better things were coming.

After graduating from seminary, I became chaplain at a children's home where my congregation consisted of about a hundred children and teenagers who couldn't have cared less about keen insight and deep theology. It seemed to me that my brilliance was sailing blithely over the heads of my fidgeting congregants, so I stayed at the children's home two years and then went to a place where I assumed the trumpets would blow a bit louder.

I moved to a new mission in the Houston area with the exciting assignment of leading that mission to become a full-fledged church. I thrived on the newness of that situation and the possibility of building a new church, new relationships, and new ministries. Starting a church was a thrilling experience, all right, but it had a downside. I quickly got bogged down in some of the mechanics of church planting: writing a set of bylaws, building a sanctuary, establishing the necessary church committees, formulating a church budget, and trying to placate people on radically different ends of the theological spectrum. The church grew and became a medium-sized suburban congregation, and I settled in for the long haul. I stayed at that church for twenty years, but, somewhere along the way, I started to realize that my chance for ministerial stardom might have passed me by.

I finished my pastoral career in San Antonio, where I stayed for thirteen years. My biggest challenge there was overcoming a numbing familiarity with the church, the Bible, and the sound of my own voice. I had no trouble at all believing that the good news was *good*; my problem was believing that it was *news*. It seemed to me that I and at least some of my listeners were afflicted with the deadly problem of over-familiarity. We had sung the songs so often, heard (and preached) the biblical stories so many times, and been immersed in "church stuff" for so many years that we had lost the wonder of it all. I wrote a book titled *Making the Good News Good Again* while I was at that church primarily because I needed to hear it so much in my own life.

And then, after thirty-eight years as a pastor, I retired and turned my attention to writing. Now I spend most days at local coffee shops writing articles, books, and Bible study curriculum. I don't preach often, and the little church we attend doesn't know or care about my ministerial past. But now that I'm no longer a pastor, I've had time to look back on thirty-eight years of ministry and gain some perspective on those years.

My overwhelming feeling is one of gratitude. I'm grateful for those country folks in Andice who endured the immaturity of a starry-eyed seminary student and loved him in his foolishness. I'm grateful for those children, teenagers, and cottage parents at the children's home who sat as still as they could while I rambled on about things they could not possibly understand. I'm grateful for that church in Houston, which allowed me to make mistakes, loved my family and me unreservedly, and shaped me into a better person and pastor. And I'm grateful for that church in San Antonio that was full of smart, creative, delightful people who challenged me to become smarter, more creative, and more delightful myself. I look back on my years of ministry with fond memories and unabashed gratitude. I am, of all pastors, most blessed.

But, when I look back on my ministry, I realize that "trumpets in the morning" doesn't capture my experience. I'm guessing that phrase doesn't capture the experience of most people who have served in ministry positions for a long time. And I'm afraid that if we expect a life of ministry to be a "trumpets in the morning" experience, we are setting ourselves up for disappointment.

The truth is, some mornings the trumpet doesn't sound, or if it does sound, you can't hear it.

The truth is, a life in ministry is hard, lonely, and full of conflict and stress.

The truth is, ministry is not for wimps, and if you sign on to be a minister, you'd better go into it with your eyes wide open.

The truth is, some days you will long to be a forest ranger, insurance salesperson, or lighthouse keeper—anything but a minister of the gospel of Jesus Christ.

But, in spite of its hardships, ministry is full of meaning, purpose, and, at least some days, joy. God *does* meet us in the hard places, and God *does* give strength when our strength is gone. We are not without resources when we try to do the hard work of ministry. Those who are with us are more than those who are with them, as Elisha told his servant boy (2 Kings 6:15-17).

So I'm calling this book *Bugles in the Afternoon.* When it's the hottest time of the day and the promise of the morning has faded and the solace of night has not yet arrived, we hear the muted but unmistakable bleat of a bugle. The sound of that bugle reminds us that there is still work to be done and good news to be proclaimed. It reminds us that God is still alive and well and calling us to be faithful right where we are. And it reminds us that God will give us all we need to get the job done.

On the more-than-likely chance that you have picked up this book because you are tired of ministry, tired of Christian people, tired of church politics, tired of the same old songs and Bible stories, tired of the silence and absence of God, tired of life as it is, I can only offer you the perspective of one who at least has walked a mile in your shoes. I don't have many airtight answers to give you, but I do have a sympathetic heart for your situation.

I will speak out of my own experience and hope that maybe my experience will intersect with yours. And I will hope and pray that beyond my words you will catch the faint sound of a bugle blowing in the lonely afternoon of your ministry, a bugle calling you to renewed faith and service.

Chapter 1

LIFE UNDER THE JUNIPER TREE: EXPLORING THE SHAPE OF MODERN MINISTRY

The biblical translators can't agree on exactly which kind of plant the prophet Elijah was sitting under when he had his "meltdown." Some say it was a "broom bush." Others call it a "broom tree." The translators of the King James Version call it a "juniper tree." Whatever kind of tree or bush it was, Elijah was in bad shape as he sat beneath it.

The timing of the great prophet's meltdown was both strange and surprising. He had just defeated the prophets of Baal in a famous encounter on Mount Carmel. If ever Elijah should have been brimming with confidence and faith, this was the time. He had just witnessed God's power in a miraculous way and should have been on a spiritual high.

But one threat from Queen Jezebel melted Elijah's faith like an ice cream cone on an August day in Texas. She promised to do to Elijah precisely what he had just done to the prophets of Baal (kill them), and Elijah promptly lost every shred of hope and faith he possessed:

> Elijah was terrified. He got up and ran for his life. He arrived at Beer-sheba in Judah and left his assistant there. He himself went farther on into the desert a day's journey. He finally sat down

under a solitary broom bush. He longed for his own death: "It's more than enough, LORD! Take my life because I'm no better than my ancestors." He lay down and slept under the solitary broom bush. (1 Kings 19:3-5)

How did he get so depressed? What happened to the faith he so recently possessed? Why couldn't he remember the exhilarating events of the recent past? How did he slide from faith to faithlessness so quickly?

We don't know the answers to those questions, but we do know that Elijah slumping dejectedly under that juniper tree is a sad symbol of many of us who, like him, try to minister for God in the world. Like Elijah, we've had our moments. Like Elijah, we've witnessed God do miraculous things. And, like Elijah, we assumed we would never, ever wind up under a juniper tree.

But alas, here we are—depressed, discouraged, disillusioned, and not quite sure how we got where we are. Even worse, we're not quite sure what to do about it. It's bad enough to take up residence under a juniper tree; it's even worse to feel like you'll never get out from under it.

My long experience in the church has convinced me that most ministers—both professional ministers and lay ministers—spend time under the juniper tree. Those ministers who have served more than ten years in a church or other Christian group and not been depressed, discouraged, or disillusioned can hold their annual convention in a phone booth. The rest of us, if we're honest, will admit that we occasionally visit the juniper tree and then try our best to help one another.

That, I suppose, is what this book is—one juniper tree veteran telling others how he managed to survive there. You've heard the old definition of evangelism, I'm sure: "one beggar telling another beggar where to find bread." This book is one juniper tree survivor telling other juniper tree sufferers how to find hope.

In Elijah's Footsteps

As I mentioned in the introduction, I was a pastor for thirty-eight years. I served my final two churches for thirty-three of those years—twenty at a church near Houston and thirteen at a church in San Antonio. As I also mentioned, I was, of all pastors, most blessed. I was never fired from a church. I never came under fire for any major indiscretion or problem. I never had to deal with personal attacks against me. I never had a church that faced major financial problems. I never pastored a church that was declining numerically. I came to the end of my ministry with my sanity still intact, my sense of humor still in place, my belief in God still firm, and my appreciation for the church still alive and well. Anyone who has served as a minister for thirty-eight years would be thrilled to have the experience I had. It's hard not to be grateful when the good has outweighed the bad a hundred to one.

Still . . . in spite of those wonderful blessings, At times I wanted to be anything *but* the pastor of the church I served. I was never comfortable with conflict, and there were times when it seemed that conflict was present everywhere I turned. Church members were upset about doctrinal issues. Or they were angry with a church staff member. Or staff members couldn't stand each other. Or the church spent several business meetings arguing over such weighty issues as how many folding chairs to order for the fellowship hall or which window shades would best match the carpet. There were days when I felt like a referee, not a pastor.

When the church sailed into a protracted time of conflict, I started itching to be elsewhere—anywhere, in fact, but in the middle of all of that dissension. During these protracted seasons of conflict, I dreamed of doing something different, something that did not involve quarreling people. Like maybe becoming a forest ranger. Or a lighthouse keeper. I can actually pinpoint several seasons in my ministerial life when I did flirt with other possibilities.

There was the time I considered owning a bookstore. I heard about a bookstore that was available on the Strand in Galveston. Sherry and I went to Galveston, not far from where we lived at the time, to check it out. It was a nice store, but it sold mostly used books. And the location wasn't great. After seeing it, we could see why it was for sale. It probably didn't make much money. Even so, I thought to myself, it might be better than having to go to the next deacons' meeting.

Then there was the second time I considered owning a bookstore. This one was in Bandera, Texas, and, once again, Sherry and I made a trip to scope it out. It turned out to be filled with mostly cowboy books. After all, Bandera calls itself "the cowboy capital of the world," so the bookstore fit well there. But it wasn't exactly the kind of bookstore I wanted to own. I did check out the profit-loss statement of this store, and it was not a pretty picture. Even so, I reasoned, it might be better than arguing over the budget at the next church council meeting.

Then there was the bed-and-breakfast possibility that we pursued during the midst of one of the church conflict sieges. This B&B was in a classic, old brick house in Waco, near the Baylor campus, and it had a lot of appeal—until we discovered how much money they wanted for it. It was definitely out of our price range. Even so, I figured, it might be better than having to go the meeting with the angry church member who wanted to quiz me about my orthodoxy.

There was also the freelance-writer phase that presented itself as a possibility during one of my juniper tree times. I bought several books about the business of writing—books advising me how to make it as a freelancer, how to market my books, and the pleasures of the writing life. It all sounded idyllic, and I've always loved writing, so this seemed like a good possibility . . . until I got my next royalty check. That check was a major wake-up call. It reminded me that I'm not John Grisham after all. I did the math and figured out that I would have to crank out about a hundred books a year to make a living as a writer. Even so, becoming a freelance writer sounded enticing when I thought about the upcoming personnel committee meeting when we would talk about terminating our youth minister.

There were a few other phases and dreams that I won't bother to mention, but you get my drift. Though I was in really good churches with really good people and having a really "successful ministry," I became acquainted with the juniper tree. My blood pressure went up. I developed a slight hand tremor. I started experiencing periodic lower back pain. Occasionally, I had trouble sleeping. I was more irritable with my wife and kids than I wanted to be. I never had any major depression, but I did have bouts with a minor variety.

For years, I had a habit of grading each day and putting that grade in my day planner. The grade measured my emotional state on that particular day. If I was filled with joy, creativity, and good will, the day got a "10." If I was joyless, flat, and out of sorts, the day got a "1." When I look back at those planners now, I see a bunch of "5's" and "6's." Most days when I was a pastor, I wasn't exactly groveling with the turkeys, but I wasn't soaring with the eagles either.

When I look back at those planners now and see the grades I gave my days, I can't help wondering what I would have done if I had had major problems in my ministry. If, in the midst of a growing church with financial stability and spiritual unity, I gave myself "5's" and "6's," what grade would I have given myself if I'd had to deal with the trauma many ministers have to face?

I shudder to think.

A Friend under the Tree

One of the saddest things about the biblical story of Elijah under the juniper tree is the loneliness in it. He had left his assistant back in Beersheba, so there was no one around to help him bear his burden. Why would Elijah go to that juniper tree by himself? We can only speculate. Maybe he wanted to be alone so he could hear God without competing voices. Maybe he was embarrassed that a renowned prophet of God could be so depressed and wanted to hide his depression from others. Or maybe he was so distraught that the thought of human company filled him with dread. Whatever it was that prompted him, Elijah chose to sit under that tree all by himself.

I, however, had a friend with me under the tree, a friend who probably saved my ministry and my sanity. My friend was my dad's brother, Glen Edwards, a Baptist pastor for many years in Texas and Louisiana. Any time I found myself under the juniper tree, I would call him and get immediate comfort. It wasn't so much that he had answers; it was simply that he was a kindred spirit, someone who understood both me and my struggle. Any time I started sinking into the pit of despondence, Sherry would wisely say, "It might be time to give Uncle Glen a call."

Early in my ministry, I wrote him long letters, telling him I wasn't cut out to be a pastor, bemoaning the conflict I was dealing with, complaining about church members who didn't have a clue what the gospel was about, or, in a dozen other ways, telling him about my life under the juniper tree.

In short order, I always got a letter in return, written in long-hand and chock-full of memorable phrases. I put those letters in my desk drawer at the church and referred to them often when I needed encouragement. I don't have my end of the conversation anymore and don't remember what specific aspect of the juniper tree I was complaining about in my letters to him, but I still have his end of the conversation, which is really the only end worth saving.

I must have griped in one letter about how unfit I was to be a pastor in the institutional church, how I was losing my soul in trying to be a "successful" churchman. In response, Uncle Glen wrote,

Dear Jud,

I understand. In fact, I'm rather certain that my coronary problem was to some extent brought on by my living against the grain of my natural disposition and inclination for 40 years. . . .

There is a profound sadness to all of this, and it runs deeper than mere taste and personal preferences. In my mind, there is no question that we have rather much missed the mystery and wonder of the Gospel of grace and freedom and have, therefore, turned the church into a weird copy of cultural, commercial, industrial understandings and values. So much of it is plainly disconnected from anything that matters to either this present world or the one not yet but sure to come.

You wanted solutions to your frustration and not additional negative thoughts, I know, but in truth I have no easy, or, for that matter, hard solutions to offer. It is a shame that a man cannot be honest and above board with his thoughts and feelings where something could be done about it—at church! But, alas, the church is for hiding, not for revealing the inner workings of the soul.

The only way I maintained any degree of balance or sense of perspective was to read the mystics and reflective theologians and philosophers whose livelihood did not depend upon or derive from their institutional success. And I still find that regimen to be stabilizing and fortifying. Since being retired, I take no small pleasure in doing business with the great minds and sages of the years. This is pure delight when one is not required to "do anything with it."

Preach the truth, live it as you understand it and, happily, somehow what you have carried to the people will someday carry you. I promise!

We love it here. Being out of the thick of things suits both of us mightily. We have lots of friends, good things to do, a fine dog to follow me and wag his approval, books to read, thoughts to think, songs to sing, pleasantries to remember, and no complaints.

We wish you were closer. Maybe someday.

Love,
Glen

Another time I must have brought up the same notion, that I somehow didn't have the right temperament or personality to be a pastor. He wrote back,

Dear Jud,

Your temperament, personality, style, etc. will preclude you being a "successful" pastor and guarantee that you will be an authentic human being. The latter, for all of its discomfort and feelings of misfitness, is preferable to the former!

I must have been unusually depressed in another of my letters and got this brief note in reply:

Dear Jud,

Creative people suffer, and suffering people create. The church will never change until some who see it differently make it different. Hang in there and let things happen.

Now. Load up your wife and kids and come to see us. We could pool our misery and, by some strange alchemy, produce joy!

Peace,
Glen

As I recall, that's exactly what I did. I loaded up my wife and two kids
and went to Louisiana to see him. And, as predicted, we did produce
joy.

When I look back on those days I spent under the juniper tree, I
find myself feeling grateful all over again for my Uncle Glen, my wise
and gracious friend who was always willing to get under that juniper
tree with me. I wish Elijah had had someone like that. And I hope
and pray that you do, too.

I'm sure that my impetus to write this book stems, in no small
part, from the difference my Uncle Glen made in my life. He made
the juniper tree bearable for me, and if this book can do that for even
one minister of the good news, I will consider it a whopping success.

Elijah Is Everywhere

There is another motivating factor, too, in my desire to write about
discouragement and disillusionment in ministry: I keep bumping
into discouraged, disillusioned ministers everywhere I turn. I know
a young pastor who recently had to endure the horrors of an awful
church split. I know a youth minister who had several people leave
his church because they were mad at him. I know a college minister
who was relieved of his job on the campus where he had served faith-
fully for years. I know a woman who lost her ministry as a chaplain
at a retirement center and hasn't been able to find another "parish."
I know an older minister who doesn't want to retire but can't find
anyone who wants him as a pastor. And I know a fine lay couple
who recently left the church they helped start twenty-five years
ago because of the chaos and conflict in that church. It seems that
every direction I look I see a discouraged, disillusioned minister of
the gospel. From my small, random sampling, distraught ministers
outnumber happy ones.

Some statistics I saw on the website pastoralcareinc.com verify
my sense that my ministerial friends are the rule, not the exception:

- 80 percent of pastors believe their ministry has negatively affected their families.
- 90 percent feel they are inadequately trained to cope with the demands of their ministry.
- 70 percent constantly fight depression.
- 70 percent do not have someone they consider a close friend.
- 50 percent of the ministers starting out will not last five years.
- Only one out of ten ministers will actually retire as a minister.
- The profession of "pastor" is near the bottom of a survey of most-respected professions, just above "car salesman."
- 4,000 new churches begin each year and 7,000 churches close.
- More than 1,700 pastors left the ministry every month last year.
- More than 1,300 pastors were terminated by a church every month last year.
- More than 3,500 people a day left the church last year.[1]

If those statistics are anywhere near the truth, we have a crisis on our hands. Ministers of all kinds, not just pastors, are discouraged, disillusioned, and dropping out of ministry. Certainly, this is not just a modern phenomenon. All we have to do is read the New Testament to remember that church conflict and stress on church leaders were present back then, too. The apostle Paul, for example, probably experienced as much stress as any minister in our day.

But some factors have arisen in the last thirty years that have made the life of a modern minister especially perilous. I am now old enough to remember when these factors were not present, or at least not as prevalent, as they are now. I have witnessed the rise of these factors and know they have made the life of today's ministers a dangerous one indeed.

Consider seven facets of modern American culture and how they affect a person trying to minister for Jesus Christ in the modern world:

1. *The collapse of belief.* Twenty-five years ago, Walter Truett Anderson anticipated where our culture was headed:

In recent decades we have passed, like Alice slipping through the looking glass, into a new world. This postmodern world looks and feels in many ways like the modern world that preceded it: we still have belief systems that gave form to the modern world, and indeed we also have remnants of many of the belief systems of premodern societies. If there is anything we have plenty of, it is belief systems. But we also have something else: a growing suspicion that all belief systems—all ideas about human reality—are social constructions.[2]

In other words, the notion of absolute, eternal, divinely given truth has collapsed for most people. People feel that their beliefs are human constructions that can be changed as the need arises. There is the perception that beliefs arise from within people, not from some external Source.

The cover of an *Utne Reader* several years ago captured this facet of our society perfectly. Under the heading "Designer God," it showed a smiling boy with outstretched hands. He was wearing a yarmulke and locks of a Hasidic Jew, a Buddhist monk's robe, and a Christian cross. If you looked at him closely, you could also see two necklaces—one a yin-yang symbol from Taoism and the other a star and crescent from Islam. The article's subtitle asks, "In a mix-and-match world, why not create your own religion?"[3]

The assumption behind that question is that we each create our own beliefs, cobble together a mix-and-match religion that works for us, and use that religion to navigate our way through a treacherous world.

Enter, then, the minister of the gospel, trying to convince these people that the word of God is absolute, eternal, and divine and that they should build their lives around it. Talk about butting your head against an immovable rock! Trying to convince modern people in a mix-and-match culture to buy into permanent, immutable truths is guaranteed to produce both frustration and stress.

2. *A shrinking attention span.* There was a time, believe it or not, when Americans would listen to a politician or preacher for hours. That was well before my time, but in the 1800s, people listened to a speech or sermon for longer than we now think humanly possible.

No sane politician or preacher would attempt to speak that long today. The people in our audience have been shaped by thirty-minute sitcoms and thirty-second commercials. They're used to pointing their cursor at something, clicking, and getting instant results. Any person wanting to communicate with modern people had better be ready to say it quick and keep it light.

Enter, then, the minister of the gospel, charged with the task of teaching people about a long obedience in the same direction, trying to persuade people to slowly and patiently build a life that has some depth, maturity, and holiness. In a world wanting easy answers and quick fixes, the minister who tries to stay true to the age-old qualities of Christian discipleship is destined to be mostly ignored by the masses.

3. *Distrust of authority.* There was a time when ministers were put on pedestals and held in the highest esteem. If the minister said it, it was true. If the minister advocated it, we should support it, too. But the pendulum has swung completely in the opposite direction today. Ministers are seen as dogmatic, pious, and pretentious, and everything they say is suspect. I'm not surprised that pastors ranked only a notch above car salesmen in that poll of most-respected people. That's the mood of our day. Anyone in a position of power is looked upon with suspicion.

Enter, then, into this suspicious culture, the minister of the gospel, trying her best to teach her class, trying his best to serve the students on that college campus, trying her best to be a faithful shepherd to the flock she tends, and being looked at with wary eyes. No matter how hard those ministers try, or how sincere and genuine they are as people, they can't rise above suspicion. It's enough to make even the finest minister want to quit.

4. *The desire to be entertained.* Our society worships at the shrine of entertainment. Everything now has to be "fun"—including church. Youth ministers want to have a fun youth ministry. Children's ministers want the kids to have fun at church. Even pastors try to liven up worship by bringing object lessons or dressing up as a biblical hero to make the sermon "come alive." In a culture that

worships entertainment and entertainers, we know that the church can't survive if it is not "fun."

Frankly, I understand that. I've been in enough boring, overbearing, beat-you-over-the-head church services that having a little fun at church sounds appealing. But the stress this preoccupation with entertainment puts on ministers is almost unbearable. They feel they must be funny, winsome, and engaging all the time. Church leadership is reduced to having a good personality and making people laugh. Those called to declare the whole gospel know that parts of it are not "fun" and that it's going to be a hard sell in our kind of world.

So, into this fun-seeking world, enter the minister of the gospel, called to say hard, demanding things to people who only want to have a good time. When people primarily want to party, how can you hope to talk to them about a cross?

5. *Multiculturalism.* That first church I pastored in central Texas was the only church in town. In that community, you either went to our Baptist church or you went to the Presbyterian church down the road that only had services every other Sunday. That was it: Baptist every week or Presbyterian every other week. But either place you went, you found the same kinds of people—white, Anglo-Saxon, Protestant, heterosexual Texas farmers and their families. It was a homogeneous culture that looked askance at anyone who was "different." That's the way it was in most churches forty years ago.

Fast-forward forty years, and the scene has changed dramatically. Now our communities, schools, and churches are filled with diversity. It's no longer only a choice between the Baptists or the Presbyterians. There's a Believer's Fellowship down the road, a synagogue around the corner, and a mosque not a stone's throw away. And even in our own church, we have people of different color, sexual orientation, economic status, and theological persuasion. Not everyone at church is exactly like we are anymore.

That means our churches have become breeding grounds for dissension. It's easier to get along with people just like us than it is to get along with all of these strange folks who have washed up on the shores of our churches. Anyone in a place of leadership in one of these multicultural situations is destined for conflict. And, these days, that's nearly every minister in any town with more than five thousand people.

Enter the minister of the gospel into this world of different cultures, beliefs, and ways of coming at life. It's a confusing snarl of humanity, and anyone brash enough to step into the middle of it may get hurt. Multiculturalism is exciting and positive, but it does produce new challenges for both the church and its leaders.

6. *Obsession with technology.* Believe it or not, when I started my ministry, I didn't have a computer or a cell phone. There was no e-mail, Twitter, or Facebook. If you wanted to communicate with someone back in those days, you met them for coffee, called them on the phone, or wrote them a letter. It sounds quaint and archaic now.

By the time I finished my ministry, I spent a good part of most days on my computer—writing a sermon, answering e-mails, ordering a book from Amazon, or doing research for a book or article. At the end of some of those days, I would wonder what I used to do with all the hours I now spent at the computer.

Our culture has become obsessed with technology and, no doubt, has reaped many benefits from computers, televisions, cell phones, and all of the amazing contraptions now available to us. But the danger inherent in technology is that it is not personal. It is one step removed from a flesh-and-blood encounter with another human being, which is the very heart of Christian ministry.

I seriously doubt that Jesus would have wanted to be on television, had they had television in his day. I doubt that he would have sent e-mails expounding his truth, had they had e-mail in his day. And I'm pretty certain that he wouldn't have tweeted the Sermon on the Mount, had they had Twitter in ancient Palestine. He would have wanted to see, touch, and hear people—live and in person—because that's how real ministry happens.

Enter into that technological society the minister of the gospel. He or she wants to be personal, wants to know people intimately, wants to get deeper than technology will allow, but no one wants to go there. They would rather "tweet" than meet for a cup of coffee.

7. *A shallow concept of success.* The measure of success in the modern church and most other Christian ministries is the same

measure of success employed by the corporate world. We Christians have borrowed our concept of success from big business.

That means we want to have more people, more money, bigger buildings, an attentive and impressive staff, and attractive programs that will help our institution grow. Nearly every church or para-church organization in America has those goals as a measure of success. And anyone who has ever led a Christian institution would probably agree that more people is better than fewer people, bigger buildings are better than little buildings, an attentive and impressive staff is better than an inattentive and shoddy staff, and attractive programs are better than lousy programs. Given a choice between growth and stagnation, anyone in a place of leadership would vote for growth.

But this puts ministers in a bind. They didn't sign on to run an institution; they signed on to celebrate the good news of the gospel and to encourage others to do the same. They didn't get their call from the church; they got it from God. And when those two entities are at cross-purposes, ministers feel compelled to go with God. Talk about stress! The church has one concept of success; God, as the minister understands God, has another concept of success; and the minister is caught squarely in the middle.

Here's the modern minister trying to please the church council and God at the same time. It's a no-win situation, and the minister spends a lot of sleepless nights wrestling with the tension.

The Perfect Storm

Add up those seven factors and see what you get. In a culture where belief has collapsed, attention spans have shrunk, authority is suspect, entertainment is worshiped, multiculturalism presents new challenges, technology is rampant, and success is measured only in numbers, what you get is a ton of stress on anyone trying to be a faithful minister of Jesus Christ.

We have sailed into the "perfect storm" of discouragement and disillusionment for Christian leaders. That's why those statistics I quoted earlier are no surprise. It's a tough time to be a minister of the gospel of Jesus Christ, and many will decide to opt out. Life is too short to be miserable, and it seems ridiculous to keep hitting your head against immovable cultural walls.

If you decide to stay in church ministry or some other kind of Christian work, I don't think you can expect things to get easier any time soon. Those seven factors I've mentioned are not going to go away, and we're going to have to learn how to minister in a culture that, to use Jesus' memorable phrase, doesn't have "ears to hear" us. To make matters worse, even the church itself, filled with people breathing the toxic fumes of our society, doesn't have "ears to hear" us.

So strap on your seatbelt. Seek the Spirit's wisdom and courage. And let's try to figure out how to survive (dare we say thrive?) as ministers of the gospel of Jesus Christ in this kind of world.

Notes

1. Pastoralcareinc.com, "Statistics in the Ministry," http://www.pastoralcareinc.com/statistics/.

2. Walter Truett Anderson, *Reality Isn't What It Used to Be* (San Francisco: HarperSanFrancisco, 2011) 3.

3. Cited in John Suk, *Not Sure* (Grand Rapids MI: Eerdmans, 2011) 104.

Chapter 2

THE ENEMIES CIRCLING THE CITY: IDENTIFYING THE STRESSES OF MINISTRY

There was a time in biblical history when Israel was in conflict with the Arameans. The king of Aram was plotting against the people of Israel and planning a military strategy against them. But, time after time, the prophet Elisha found out about the king's plan and warned the king of Israel about it. The Aramean king was understandably both puzzled and upset about this situation and tried to find out who was supplying this "inside information" to his enemy. When one of his officers told him that the informer was Elisha, the king sent a large battalion to the city of Dothan to take care of Elisha once and for all.

The Aramean army came at night and surrounded the city. Let's pick up the biblical story there:

> Elisha's servant got up early and went out. He saw an army with horses and chariots surrounding the city. His servant said to Elisha, "Oh, no! Master, what will we do?" "Don't be afraid," Elisha said, "because there are more of us than there are of them." . . . Then the LORD opened the servant's eyes, and he saw that the mountain was full of horses and fiery chariots surrounding Elisha. (2 Kings 6:15-17)

Some mornings, when I was a pastor, I would saunter over to the French doors that led to our back yard, peer outside, and jokingly say to Sherry, "I'm pretty sure the enemy is encircling the city this morning." But, of course, I was only *half*-joking. Inevitably, when I said that, there was something I had to do that day that I dreaded. A meeting with a church member who was mad about something. A committee meeting that promised to be longer and more boring than it needed to be. A funeral that would be emotional and draining. Or a staff meeting that would be filled with unspoken tension and hostility. Most mornings in ministry, some enemy has shown up in the darkness of night and encircled our city.

I think it is important, though, that we not avert our eyes from these enemies and try to act like they're not there. The way to defeat enemies encircling our ministries is to recognize their presence and meet them head-on, trusting all the while that "there are more of us than there are of them."

When I look back on a long ministry of dealing with those enemies, I can recognize them better now than I did then. In those days, they looked so menacing outside my house in the morning, but now I see them as the paper tigers they really were. I outlasted them all, made it to a happy retirement, and wish I'd had the audacity to laugh in their faces.

In this chapter, consider with me a few of the enemies that encircle our ministries and rob us of joy.

The Stress of Constant Availability

There's something about knowing that you're constantly "on call" that adds a major stress to life. Someone asked me not long ago what I enjoy most about retirement. I said it is the feeling of "lightness" I now have. When I was a pastor, I unconsciously carried a heaviness that came primarily from knowing the phone could ring at any moment, summoning me to go to the hospital or attend to some other crisis. It's hard to enjoy a ballgame on television or take a nap on Saturday afternoon when you know that phone call is a distinct possibility.

Looking back on it now, that phone call rarely came. I can remember some occasions when I had to get up in the middle of the night to visit a hospital or rush to a family in crisis, but those occasions were rare. It wasn't that I had to go on emergency runs all the time, but the idea that I *might* have to go on them weighed on me heavily.

Every minister wants to be available. Or, maybe better said, every minister wants to have the reputation of being available. We live in dread of church members complaining that we were not available in their time of need. They went to the hospital, we imagine them saying, and we didn't visit them. They lost a loved one, and we didn't call. We have this nagging fear that, behind our back, the church is whispering, "Well, he's a decent preacher, but he's not much of a pastor." Or "She knows a lot about the Bible, but she's not much of a minister." Then they relate with a quivering voice that time we "dropped the ball" and didn't meet their need.

I remember all too vividly the time I received a call from a church member telling me that a certain person who had been attending our church was hurt that I had not visited his cousin who had been in the hospital. Never mind that I didn't know this person's cousin. Never mind that I didn't even know that his cousin had been in the hospital. The bottom line was that I was the pastor, and I had not been there in this person's time of need. I called this hurt person on the phone and asked about his cousin to try to assuage his wounded feelings and also preserve my reputation as a caring pastor. Heaven forbid that anyone start the mantra that I was a good preacher but not much of a pastor!

There's a lot of stress in having to be constantly available. It not only puts heaviness into our lives whenever we want to watch ballgames or take naps but also tempts us to have a forced, fake ministry. Instead of being genuinely interested in people, we're actually concerned about *appearing* to be genuinely interested in people. More than anything, we want to be known as caring, available ministers, and our reputation becomes more important than our ministry. I eventually came to believe that discerning people could see right through my motives and spot forced, fake ministry in a heartbeat.

There is no easy answer to this dilemma. All of these things are true: we do have to be available to people; some ministers do a poor job of "being there"; those awful phone calls do come; and part of being a minister is being willing to be available and to carry the "heaviness" that goes with that availability.

But there is a point where we become tyrannized by those realities. We become so fearful of not being available that we are obsessed with what people think of us. We become forced, fake ministers wanting to impress people with how "loving" we are. And the heaviness of being that available and that loving becomes almost unbearable.

Mark Twain once described a woman he knew as a "good woman, in the worst sense of the word." If we become obsessed with our reputation and our availability, we can easily become a "good minister, in the worst sense of the word."

The Stress of Being God's Representative

I like going to the grocery store. I know that's odd, but there's something about it that I find fun and entertaining. And I enjoy it even more now than I used to. When I was a pastor, I felt like I needed to shave and wear presentable clothes to the grocery store in case I ran into some church members—which I usually did. Now that I'm retired and have moved to another city, I venture to the grocery store unshaven, wearing shorts, a T-shirt, and sandals, knowing that no one will know me. The anonymity of it all is glorious!

There is a certain stress in feeling like God's representative in any and all situations—even in the grocery store. God's representatives never feel the freedom to let their guard down. Someone is watching to make sure they dress right, talk right, believe right, and act right. The spotlight never fades, and the pressure to appear "godly" never leaves.

In Exodus 34, we read the fascinating story of Moses on Mount Sinai. It tells us that, in the presence of God, Moses' face would start to glow. So he started putting a veil over his face. That image of a veiled Moses yields two possibilities. He might have put on that veil because his face was shining so much that it hurt the eyes of the

Israelites who beheld it. Moses might have worn that veil as a kindness to those who had to look at him.

But it's also possible that he put the veil on so that the people wouldn't know when he lost his glow, when he hadn't been in the presence of God. That veil could have been Moses' way of protecting the eyes of the people, but it also could have been his way of protecting his own reputation as a holy person who was always glowing for God.

It is tempting to put a veil on so that people can't see us clearly. That way, they don't know if we've lost our glow or not. That way, we can maintain our image as God's representative and keep anyone from thinking we might actually be a normal human being who occasionally loses the glow.

That veil also keeps people from discovering how little we actually know. Part of being God's representative is that we supposedly know things other people don't know. We're ordained ministers, which must mean that we know God better than ordinary people know God. We also know about the Bible, church history, other religions, psychological theories and techniques, theories of the atonement, our church's bylaws, and Robert's Rules of Order. Being a minister means we know things ordinary people don't know.

For that reason, when someone comes to us and asks a question from way out in left field—"When was Hezekiah king of Israel?" or "What exactly do the Muslims believe?"—we can't bring ourselves to tell the truth: "Frankly, I have no idea." Instead, we invoke our finest ministerial voice and offer some cliché that we hope gives the impression of certainty. We wouldn't want anyone to think that we, as a representative of God, could possibly be ignorant about something.

But let's be honest: trying to be God's representative has produced some very strange people. It has created ministers who are tight, tense, fake, and unpleasant to be around. They pride themselves on being ministers of God, but ordinary people avoid them like they have leprosy—or piety!

In her fine book *Leaving Church*, Barbara Brown Taylor writes,

While I knew plenty of clergy willing to complain about high expectations and long hours, few of us spoke openly about the

toxic effects of being identified as the holiest person in a congregation. Whether this gift was conferred by those who recognized our
gifts for ministry or was simply extended by them as a professional
courtesy, it was equally hard on the honorees. Those of us who
believed our own press developed larger-than-life swaggers and
embarrassing patterns of speech, while those who did not suffered
lower-back pain and frequent bouts of sleeplessness. Either way,
we were deformed.[1]

The stress of trying to be God's representative does deform us. For
that reason, I think back to something my Uncle Glen said in one
of his letters: Wouldn't it be better to fail at becoming a "successful"
minister if it meant succeeding at becoming an authentic human
being?

The Stress of Success

Weighing heavy on any minister is the constant strain of institutional
success. True, we want people to know God, celebrate the good news,
learn to live in peace with others, and become stewards of creation.
But, just as true, we want worship attendance to increase, offerings to
grow, and the institution we lead to thrive. If we're honest, we have
to admit that sometimes that second set of goals preempts the first.

I spent most of my ministry in a state of semi-denial—resolutely
denying that I was the captain of an institutional ship. I chafed under
the idea that I was a religious CEO whose primary job was "running
an organization." No, no, no! I was a pastor, called to something
higher and holier than "running an organization."

Years ago, I marked this passage in one of Eugene Peterson's
books because it so aptly captured my call and my view of ministry:

We set out to do something different. We set out to risk our lives
in a venture of faith. We committed ourselves to a life of holiness.
At some point we realized the immensity of God and of the great
invisibles that socket into our arms and legs, into bread and wine,
into our brains and our tools, into mountains and rivers giving
them meaning, destiny, value, joy, beauty, salvation. We responded
to a call to convey these realities in word and sacrament and to give

leadership to a community of faith in such a way that connected what the men and women, children and youth in this community are doing in their work and play with what God is doing in mercy and grace. In the process, we learned the difference between a profession or craft, and a job.[2]

That said it for me. I didn't want a job; I wanted a profession or craft. No, even more than that, I wanted a calling. To me, being a pastor was a sacred calling to a holy task.

That high view of my calling, though, kept running into sticky, unpleasant, organizational realities: Bible study attendance was sagging, the sound system in the sanctuary kept cutting out, some of our young adults were heading off to other churches, and the toilet in the women's bathroom kept clogging. More than once I prayed, "Deliver me, O God, from such mundane matters, and let me attend to high and holy things!"

But those mundane matters wouldn't go away because, try as I might to deny it, our church *was* an institution. So we tried to shore up Bible study attendance, called someone to fix the sound system, enhanced our programming for young adults, and got a plumber to unclog that toilet. Sometimes we ministers have to grit our teeth and attend to those things so that we can then turn our attention to high and holy things. Or, perhaps, those mundane matters *are* high and holy things!

I simply know that there is a lot of stress in trying to maintain a successful organization. We want things to "blow and go" because people are knocking down the doors to get into our exciting place of ministry. We want members to brag on "how the church is growing" because of our dynamic leadership. That's all normal and understandable. Institutional success is wonderful when we have it and awful when we don't. And it is always one of those enemies that shows up in the middle of the night to worry us.

But I'm still idealistic enough to believe the truth of that Eugene Peterson passage. I still believe we're not *primarily* doing a job, running an organization, and growing an institution; *primarily*, we're responding to a divine call and risking our lives in a venture of faith.

The Stress of Conflict

I mentioned earlier that conflict management was never my strong suit. It was the presence of conflict more than any other factor that propelled me to think about owning a bookstore, running a bed and breakfast, or becoming a freelance writer. I assumed, when I became a pastor, that I would occasionally have to deal with conflict, but I never assumed that dealing with conflict would become my primary task.

But many days, that's what I felt. I wanted to focus on positive things like sermon preparation, prayer, and pastoral care, but, on more days than I care to remember, I was forced to focus on negative things like upset church members, contentious committee meetings, and staff problems. Some days I felt like I needed to strap on a suit of armor before I headed to the church.

The frustrating thing about this, of course, is that we think Christians should be above petty conflict and silly bickering. Surely, people who know Jesus and are led by the Spirit should not be guilty of gossip and backbiting. Surely, Christian people have been so transformed by the grace of God that they're above such worldly vices.

If we believe that, we haven't read the New Testament, and we haven't been in a church or other Christian organization very long. If we ever wander into unrealistic expectations for the church, all we have to do is reread Paul's letters to the Corinthians. He penned the great "love chapter" to those people primarily because they needed it so desperately! That church was full of petty, contentious people, and Paul, as he was prone to do, confronted them head-on. Some of us who minister in contemporary churches would almost swear we've landed in Corinth.

The number one reason ministers leave churches, I'm convinced, is conflict. They get tired of fighting, tired of wrangling over silly issues, tired of power struggles, tired of trying to change a congregational system that has been broken for decades. Finally, something pushes them over the edge, and they decide to minister elsewhere— or find a bookstore or bed and breakfast to run. Life is too short to spend it fighting with fellow Christians. Our society is filled with devoted, capable men and women who entered the ministry with excitement and expectation and now find themselves so sick of the church they can't even bring themselves to attend anymore.

They thought church people were better than they are. They thought they could handle any conflict that came along. And they thought God could work miracles in even the most contentious congregation. None of those things happened, and they quietly—or not so quietly—moved on.

I will shortly devote an entire chapter to dealing with conflict, so I'll have much more to say about this topic. Let's just admit now that conflict in our church or other religious organization is one of the major stresses in ministers' lives.

The Stress of Too Many Hats

When I was in seminary, a pastor of a large church near campus told me I needed to be able to do two things to be a good pastor: I needed to be able to preach, and I needed to love people. I took comfort in that counsel because it seemed both simple and attainable. I assumed I could learn to preach, and I did love people. Maybe I truly had what it took to be a pastor.

But when I actually became a pastor a few years later, I realized that, while it was important to be a good preacher and to love people, much more than that was expected of me. In fact, I soon realized that I had at least eleven hats I was expected to wear:

• *Preacher.* I was expected to have a fresh, inspired, carefully prepared sermon each week. So I read countless books on preaching and listened to many renowned preachers to try to learn the craft of preaching.

• *Caregiver.* I was expected to provide pastoral care to people in the church and even in the community. So I visited people in the hospital and in nursing homes, performed weddings and funerals, and tried to be available in other situations where pastoral care was needed.

• *Friend.* I quickly realized, though, that the people in my church wanted more than a professional caregiver. They wanted a friend. They wanted someone who knew them and their children, who would attend ballgames and dance recitals, who would have coffee with them at the local café. If I was going to be a good pastor, I needed to be a friend and, as that pastor told me, love people.

• *Counselor.* I needed to have some counseling skills. People with problems would come to see me, and I needed to know how to help those in the midst of a troubled marriage, those grieving the loss of a loved one, those whose children were driving them crazy—people, in other words, having to deal with life in the real world.

• *Business Executive.* I discovered (though I did attempt to deny it) that I was viewed as the CEO of an institution. Church members expected me to know something about church construction, finance, staff management, committee structure, marketing, and the demographics of our neighborhood. To put it bluntly, I was expected to know how to "run a church."

• *Visionary.* People expected me to cast a vision for our church. They measured my leadership by how well I could set goals and then inspire the church to meet those goals. On more than one occasion, I had church members complain, "Our church doesn't know where it's going," and I always took that as a criticism of my leadership. A worthy pastor was expected to dream big dreams and get the church to chase those dreams.

• *Boss.* I was head of the staff at our church, which meant I was the supervisor of other ministers. They looked to me for wisdom and advice, and every year I sat down with them to evaluate their ministry. Though I never felt comfortable in the role, "boss" was how many in the church viewed me.

• *Scholar.* As a pastor, I was supposed to be schooled in Scripture, church history, how to serve the Lord's Supper, how to baptize a person, and how to translate both Greek and Hebrew. After all, I had been to seminary. Surely that made me more scholarly than the typical pew-person.

• *Evangelist.* I was expected to share the gospel with those who didn't believe. If our baptisms didn't measure up to last year's number, it was not a good sign. It meant that both the church and its pastor had not been zealous enough in winning others to Christ.

• *Public Relations Expert.* Beyond evangelism, I had a role as "face of the church." I needed to pray at the local Rotary Club meeting, attend community prayer breakfasts, serve in denominational capacities, and generally represent our church to the world. I needed to be friendly, engaging, and involved, so that people would think well of our church.

• *Writer.* I quickly realized that I had to do quite a bit of writing in my role as a pastor. I had to write sermons, newsletter articles, letters to church members, columns for the local newspaper, and, in my case, books that I hoped might get published someday. I went to several writers' conferences and read many books trying to enhance my writing skills.

When I look now at those eleven hats, I realize that I wore only four of them well. I was average in three of those areas. And I was absolutely lousy in four of them. In other words, of the eleven hats I was forced to wear as a pastor, I was mediocre or poor at seven of them. When I put those seven hats on, they didn't fit. It's a wonder those churches didn't fire me and find a pastor who could wear those hats better than I could.

Of course, there's a lot of stress in trying to wear hats that don't fit. It makes you do things you don't want to do and be things you don't want to be. And I'm guessing no pastor in the world can effectively wear all eleven hats. We ministers are destined to fail at a number of duties people expect us to perform.

The Stress of Wreckage

Almost every day we ministers have to gaze upon the wreckage of the world, the wreckage of people we know and love. Peterson describes it like this:

The sheer quantity of wreckage is appalling: wrecked bodies, wrecked marriages, wrecked careers, wrecked plans, wrecked families, wrecked alliances, wrecked friendships, wrecked prosperity. We avert our eyes. We try not to dwell on it. We whistle in the dark. We wake up in the morning hoping for health and love, justice and success, build quick mental and emotional defenses against the inrush of bad news, and try to keep our hopes up. And then some kind of crash or other puts us or someone we care about in a pile of wreckage. Newspapers document the ruins with photographs and headlines. Our own hearts and journals fill in the details. Are there any promises, any hopes that are exempt from the general carnage? It doesn't seem so.[3]

Walking amid all that carnage is bound to take a toll on ministers—and it does. I remember well the event that showed me how much of a toll that wreckage exacted of me. It was Thursday, my day off. As we usually did on Thursday, Sherry and I had been to breakfast at our favorite restaurant and then to the bookstore to do some browsing. We got home mid-morning and checked our phone messages (this was before the advent of cell phones).

There was a message from my secretary telling me to call the church as soon as I could. I called her but wasn't prepared for the shocking news: a fourteen-year-old boy in our church had committed suicide that morning. His distraught parents had called the church and asked for me to come to their house as soon as possible. I changed clothes and was there in less than thirty minutes.

I don't remember all the details of the next few days. I know I visited several times with the parents and sister of the boy. I know I planned a memorial service for him. I know we had that service at our church and that it was attended by several hundred teenagers who were Darren's friends. And I know I felt inadequate to say words on such an occasion and asked God to use my feeble efforts to bring comfort and hope to all who came to that service.

But I also remember what happened after the service. I wanted to be alone after the pressure of the past few days and decided to get out the night of the funeral and take my usual three-mile run through the neighborhood. I always enjoyed these runs and found them to be good therapy. Only this night, as I took off through the neighborhood, I couldn't run. I had absolutely no energy. I was on empty and had to be content to walk those three miles. The events of the previous few days had siphoned all the energy out of me. I was emotionally and physically drained, and it would be several days before I had the energy to run again.

Granted, that was not typical wreckage. The suicide of a teenager is about as bad as it gets, and most days I didn't have to cope with that kind of pain. But the experience showed me that wreckage does do damage to a minister. Having to walk in the midst of wreckage day after day leaves us emotionally, physically, and even spiritually spent.

Deal with that wreckage long enough and you might not be able to mount up with wings as eagles or run and not be weary. You might be happy just to walk and not faint.

Not an Ideal World

In the ideal world, we would wake up every morning to the sound of trumpets. They would summon us to a life of meaningful ministry and redemptive relationships. We would leap out of bed, anxious to be about the Lord's business and thrilled to be doing exactly what we are doing where we are doing it.

And, thank God, some mornings that does happen. We hear the trumpets, rise to greet a new day, and feel fulfilled and happy in our work. When we have those mornings, we should appreciate them and thank God for them because we won't get them every day.

Some mornings—maybe more than we care to admit—we rise not to the sound of trumpets but to the sound of the enemy shuffling around outside and making ominous noises. I've mentioned six enemies I encountered regularly in my ministry, and you can probably add some of your own to the list. Our response to those enemies is often like the response of Elisha's servant boy—a mixture of fear, dread, and confusion. "Oh, no! Master, what shall we do?" we cry.

One thing I could do, I realized, was look those enemies in the eye and try to understand them. And when I did that, I saw that they were propped up by some illusions and false assumptions. It's not that the enemies weren't there; they most assuredly were. But I was giving them more power than they deserved. Those enemies looked more ferocious than they actually were because they were feeding off the illusions I had created in my own mind.

If I could get rid of those illusions—if I could literally become disillusioned—I had a chance to reduce my enemies to manageable proportions. And if I could reduce them to manageable proportions, those that were on my side would be far greater than those on their side.

One of the best ways we deal with the enemies who show up at night and strike fear into our hearts is to recognize how dependent they are on our illusions. In the next chapter, let's turn our attention to the illusions that feed our fears and try to determine what we can do to get rid of them.

Notes

1. Barbara Brown Taylor, *Leaving Church* (San Francisco: HarperSanFrancisco, 2006) 3.

2. Eugene Peterson, *Working the Angles* (Grand Rapids MI: Eerdemans, 1987) 7.

3. Ibid., 15.

Chapter 3

VANITY OF VANITIES: EXPERIENCING THE JOY OF DISILLUSIONMENT

There is one book in the Bible that, at least implicitly, extols the virtues of disillusionment. The book of Ecclesiastes is the chronicle of one man's disillusionment and how it led to his salvation. As such, Ecclesiastes is the perfect book for learning how to deal with the enemies that greet us every morning.

When you read Ecclesiastes, you get the impression that the writer was handed a script telling him how to experience a joyful life. He assumed that if he would just follow these proven steps, he would be happy and his life would be a success. The script given to him evidently had four primary words on it, all beginning with the letter "W."

He should seek *wisdom*, the script said, so he gives himself to the pursuit of knowledge and learning. The entire book chronicles his search for wisdom. But the search is futile:

> I said to myself, Look here, I have grown much wiser than any who ruled over Jerusalem before me. My mind has absorbed great wisdom and knowledge. But when I set my mind to understand wisdom, and also to understand madness and folly, I realized that this too was just wind chasing. Remember: In much wisdom is much aggravation; the more knowledge, the more pain. (1:16-18)

The more he chased wisdom, the more frustrated he became. Chasing wisdom, he discovered, was like chasing the wind.

So he tried *wine*. If wisdom was a dead-end street, maybe wine, pleasure, and fun would take him somewhere:

> I said to myself, Come I will make you experience pleasure; enjoy what is good! But this too was pointless! Merriment, I thought, is madness; pleasure, of no use at all. I tried cheering myself with wine and by embracing folly—with wisdom still guiding me— until I might see what is really worth doing in the few days that human beings have under heaven. (2:1-3)

Wine, pleasure, and the pursuit of fun didn't take him where he wanted to go either. As it turned out, they were not really worth doing in the few days that human beings have under heaven.

So he turned his attention to *work*:

> I took on great projects: I built houses for myself, planted vine-yards for myself. I made gardens and parks for myself, planting every kind of fruit tree in them. I made reservoirs for myself to water my lush groves. I acquired male servants and female servants; I even had slaves born in my house. I also had great herds of cattle and sheep, more than any who preceded me in Jerusalem. (2:4-7)

Here, we assume, is a successful man! Here is someone who has found in his business life and work accomplishments the satisfaction he has always craved. But if we think that work was his long-sought salvation, we need to think again: "But when I surveyed all that my hands had done, and what I had worked so hard to achieve, I realized that it was pointless—a chasing after the wind" (2:11).

Finally, he tried *wealth*:

> I amassed silver and gold for myself, the treasures of kings and provinces. I acquired male and female singers for myself, along with every human luxury, treasure chests galore! So I became far greater than all who preceded me in Jerusalem. (2:8-9)

But, as with the other items in his life-script, wealth proved to be vanity. The word that he repeats over and over is that word, "vanity," also translated "pointless" in the Common English Bible. Everything on his list—wisdom, wine, work, and wealth—had been tried and found wanting. They were all a futile chasing after the wind.

The writer of Ecclesiastes was experiencing disillusionment with a capital "D." He discarded advice, assumptions, family folklore, long-cherished beliefs, and much-beloved theology, and that is a most painful process. But here is where it finally led him: "So this is the end of the matter; all has been heard. Worship God and keep God's commandments because this is what everyone must do" (12:13). On the far side of his disillusionment was a renewed interest in following God. There was one more "W" he needed to try: *worship*.

It is always both painful and liberating to face our illusions. Those enemies encircling my city every morning were there, I realized, because my illusions had empowered them to be there. Like the writer of Ecclesiastes, I needed to become disillusioned if I was going to conquer them, if I hoped to allow God to function as God in my ministry.

The six enemies I mentioned in the previous chapter looked especially terrifying because they were supported and energized by what I perceive to be some common ministerial illusions. Just in case you have some of the same enemies I had, and just in case your enemies are fed by some of the same illusions I tried to live up to, I'll run through a quick checklist of ministerial illusions that are guaranteed to make us miserable.

Availability and the Illusion of Living Up to Expectations

Feeding the first enemy—that we must be available at all times to all people—is this illusion: *I must meet everyone's expectations all the time.* Anyone who has been in a position of ministry for long knows that people have high expectations of their ministers. As I mentioned in the last chapter, we are expected to wear a lot of hats and wear them well.

We are expected to be there when people are sick or, in the case of the church member I mentioned in the last chapter, when someone's

cousin is sick. We are expected to have just the right words for people
who have lost a loved one, are getting ready to be married, or have
a teenager in drug rehab. Those of us who preach are expected to
share a creative and relevant message every Sunday. We are actually
expected to be proficient in wearing all eleven of the hats I previously
delineated, so we try hard to meet those expectations.

I think it's fair to say that most ministers want to please others.
We want people to like us, and we want to be held in high esteem.
It might not be stretching it too much to say that we ministers are
happiest when people approve of us and most miserable when they
don't. A rational part of our brain knows we can't possibly meet
everyone's expectations, but we still try. And the harder we try to be
available, caring, responsive, sensitive, pastoral, and all the other fine
ministerial qualities, the "heavier" our ministry becomes.

Tied into this desire to meet people's expectations all the time is
the not-so-pleasant truth that most ministers are "unblessed." Because
we have never felt blessed and accepted by God, we desperately try to
get that blessing and acceptance from others. Myron Madden once
commented that those who can't accept the atonement are destined
to repeat it. If we can't accept God's acceptance of us, we have to
repeat the atonement through endless attempts to be caring and
available. We're like ministerial hamsters frantically running on that
treadmill in the cage and getting nothing for our efforts but fatigue.

In his book *Come to the Party*, Karl Olsson observes,

It would be unscientific and unfair to conclude that all or most
clergymen are unblessed children who seek to compensate for their
lack of favor by working terribly hard at being good. But if I draw
on my own experience, I have to conclude that many ministers I
know and many so-called "dedicated laymen" are unblessed. They
may deserve a goat and a party, but they lack the security to ask for
it. Hence they wear themselves out in a tiresome and unrewarding
round of activities. They stay near the father and carry out their
work under his nose, but they are never very happy, and when
anyone is happy around them, they feel frustrated and envious.[1]

If we ministers could ever come to the party and know for certain that we are held in the gracious hands of a loving God, if we could ever become convinced that everything we do in ministry is not to earn God's love but because we already have it, we wouldn't have to try so hard to please others. A relaxed spirit of freedom would start bubbling up within us, allowing us to serve and minister with a new "lightness."

Freed from the tyranny of expectations and availability, we could finally enjoy what we do. Yes, we would respond when the calls come. Yes, we would try to be there when people need us. And yes, we would sometimes grumble when we had to leave the ballgame to go to the hospital.

But, embraced by a God who has numbered us among the blessed, we would not be dismayed if someone happened to be disappointed in us. Nor would we be crushed if someone declared that we haven't lived up to their expectations. We would no longer have the illusion that we can be everything people want us to be. Even if the people in our church or ministry found us wanting, we could still relax into a God who, incredibly, finds us worthy and delightful.

One of my heroes and role models in ministry was a priest I read about years ago. He ministered in a parish fraught with problems and conflict. He did his best, but his best wasn't good enough. His congregation eventually got up a petition listing his faults and demanding his resignation. Upon hearing of the petition, this country priest tracked it down—and signed it himself.

You will *not* meet everyone's expectations. Someone will find you inadequate and incompetent. The sooner you sign that petition, the freer you will be.

Being God's Representative and the Illusion of the Perfect Witness

The second stress I mentioned in the previous chapter—having to be God's perfect representative even in the grocery store—is buttressed by a second illusion I discovered within me. It was something I heard so early in life that I assumed it must be written in Scripture: *I am the only Bible some people will ever read.*

If that is true, I'm afraid those "some people" are in big trouble. I know myself well enough to know that I'm not a particularly winsome Bible. And if that illusion is true, I know that I am in trouble, too. It means I must put on a mask and appear to be much better than I really am. It means I must become that forced, fake minister who turns discerning people off with his goodness. I must become a "good minister, in the worst sense of the word."

I have always found it revealing that the one group that Jesus couldn't stomach was the religious leaders of his day. We tend to paint the scribes and Pharisees as villains in our sermons and Sunday school lessons, but I don't think that's an accurate portrayal. I think the scribes and Pharisees were men who loved God, revered Scripture, practiced morality, and wanted to protect the truth. I'm certain that they were held up as role models for Jewish children.

But Jesus reserved his harshest criticism for these men and had nothing good to say about them. When you look at his criticism, it basically comes down to this: The scribes and Pharisees believed they were the only Bible some people would ever read. They became smug ambassadors of the Holy, proud of their piety, and critical of anyone who couldn't measure up to their lofty standards. In short, in trying to be holy, they lost their humanity. And Jesus did everything in his power to try to deflate their egos and bring them back to reality. There is nothing more unbearable than a good person convinced of his goodness.

In *Come to the Party*, Olsson writes about the necessity of ministers climbing down from the perch of holiness, piety, and self-denial and claiming their humanity. He describes this as a death that most ministers will not want to experience—one he struggled with personally:

> This recognition of my humanity—my willingness to accept in myself the whole range of frailties flesh is heir to and to present myself vulnerably to the world—is my death and my dying. It is not to be humble or modest or unassuming; it is not to lie about my gifts or to lie about anything. It is to be real, to be myself. If I am the apostle Paul, it is to be Paul: bristly, sensitive, neurotic, angry, warm, loving, grateful, creative, joyous, rhapsodic. If I am

Augustine, it is to be Augustine: volcanic, profound, at once celestial and terrestrial, at once erotic and ecstatic, at once the burning intellect and luminous heart. Death means being where I am. It means not donning masks or climbing on stilts, but being incorrigibly what I am.[2]

I marked that passage in *Come to the Party* many years ago but, regrettably, never lived it very well. I remained an expert at donning masks and climbing on stilts. The illusion of being a perfect representative of God, of having to be the only Bible some people would ever read, kept me from being as real as I should have been.

The good news, of course, is that I am most assuredly *not* the only Bible people will ever read. God has such a variety of ways of touching people—through the Bible itself, through births and deaths and job losses, through books and movies and songs, through ocean waves and sunsets and hurricanes, through sins and mistakes and successes—that I stand amazed in the presence of One who can communicate in so many voices. I would like to think that, on occasion, I've been a tool God used to touch others, but I'm honest enough to admit that sometimes God probably communicated not *through* me but *in spite of* me.

It is both ignorant and arrogant to think that we are indispensable to the revelation of God. When we are prone to this common ministerial illusion, we should perhaps read Mordecai's words to Esther in the Old Testament: "In fact, if you don't speak up at this very important time, relief and rescue will appear for the Jews from another place . . ." (Esth 4:14).

When I think of this illusion of being a living Bible and the stress of constantly being God's representative to others, I think of something else Mark Twain purportedly said. He said that if he knew that someone was coming to his house with the conscious desire to do him good, he would run for his life.

I don't think the Pharisees would have understood that at all. But Jesus would have. And the older I get, the more I understand it, too.

Success and the Illusion that Bigger Is Better

Giving unnecessary strength and energy to my third enemy—the constant pressure to build a successful institution—was a third illusion: *I am responsible for growing the church because bigger is always better.*

Most Sunday nights, I was worn out from a day of preaching, attending meetings, and trying to appear holy. But I could go to bed feeling good about the day—and myself—if three things had happened that Sunday.

First, I felt good and slept well if attendance was up. If both Bible study and worship were well attended, and the numbers were up from a year earlier, I was a happy pastor. To this day, I still count the number of people who show up for worship at the little church we now attend. It's a silly and useless habit, but it's ingrained in me. Every Sunday for thirty-eight years, I counted people, and now that I no longer need to, I can't break the habit.

Second, I felt good and slept well if offerings were up. If the money counters gave me a good report of generous giving, I was a happy pastor. I knew that certain people in the church—members of the finance committee, for example—were watching that number as well. We knew that the church couldn't do much (including pay the pastor!) if we didn't meet our budget.

Third, I felt good and slept well if people had joined the church. If people had come forward at the end of the service to unite with our church, I was a happy pastor. We made it a practice in the last two churches I pastored to take pictures of new members and post them on a bulletin board at the entrance of the church. If that bulletin board was empty, it was not a good sign. But if that bulletin board was crowded with the smiling faces of people who had recently joined our church, the whole congregation felt gratified and successful. We must be doing something right, we reasoned, if all of these folks have chosen us to be their community of faith.

In other words, I was a happy pastor if the institutional markers— attendance, giving, and new members—were growing. Of course, the reverse was also true. If those things were shrinking, I was one miserable pastor, and I would have a hard time drifting off to sleep that Sunday night. I based my success as a pastor on how well our church was doing institutionally.

I knew better than that, of course. I even preached passionate sermons reminding people that the church wasn't just an institution, that the church wasn't about "buildings, budgets, and baptisms." I consistently preached that the church was about individual people, not numbers or growth. I said that the church must always look at the individual trees, not the forest. But my own feelings on Sunday night revealed what I *really* thought: we'd better grow and be "successful," or I'm going to feel like a failure as a minister.

I embraced that notion because I had been taught all my life that, when it comes to churches, bigger is always better. Bigger churches are doing a better job of reaching people. Bigger churches are doing a better job of ministering to the world. Bigger churches have more to offer people in the way of programs and opportunities. Bigger churches are bigger because the preaching is more in touch with people's needs. In effect, bigger churches have been blessed by God in a way that smaller churches haven't. And bigger churches are doing something that smaller churches need to emulate.

Though I had been taught the bigger-is-better mantra all my life, I'm not sure, now that I have time to think about it, that my teacher was Jesus. I think my teachers were capitalism, big business, and the American way. Those teachers told me that, when it comes to any institution, success is measured in size. For both Walmart and my church, the bottom line was the bottom line. And the bottom line in my particular "store" was measured by attendance, offerings, and new members. Thus, my "Sunday night syndrome" of sound sleep if the church was getting bigger—or sleeplessness if it wasn't.

As far as I can tell, though, Jesus never bought into the bigger-is-better idea. Unlike me, I doubt that he counted noses when he spoke to a crowd. And, though many of us in the church have participated in "enlargement campaigns" to make the kingdom larger, you would think when you read the Gospels that Jesus was actually leading an "ensmallment campaign."

He consistently did things that any marketing expert would call foolish. If you want to grow an organization, you don't focus most of your attention on riff-raff, women, children, and people who have no money or clout. You don't reject people like the rich young ruler who could have become the poster boy for the movement. You don't offend the religious and political power brokers of the day. You don't speak hard truths that leave people bewildered and skeptical (see John 6:66). In the Sermon on the Mount, Jesus says that his way is a narrow road that only a few people will travel, and, as his ministry unfolds, you can see why. Frankly, who wants to be this noncon- forming and "weird"?

By the end of his three-year ministry, one thing has become clear: Jesus would rather have a handful of followers who "get it" than thousands of adoring fans who don't. He wasn't interested in attracting the masses; he wanted to find a few dedicated people who were willing to die for the sake of his truth.

So it's one of the great ironies of the modern church that we now measure our success by how many people show up, how much money we can raise, and how many new people we can attract. If we have the bigger-is-better concept of church, as I always did, we got it from somewhere other than Jesus.

The sad result of the illusion that bigger is better is that we ministers become preoccupied with techniques and strategies that will make our institution grow. Instead of focusing on essential spir- itual truths that have some depth, we become managers and CEOs tinkering with superficial business models so we can attract more customers to the store.

In his book *God in the Wasteland,* David Wells writes,

> It is one of the remarkable features of contemporary church life that so many are attempting to heal the church by tinkering with its structures, its services, its public face. This is clear evidence that modernity has palmed off one of its great deceits on us, convincing us that God himself is secondary to organization and image, that the church's health lies in flow charts, its convenience, and its offerings rather than its inner life, its spiritual authenticity, the toughness of its moral intentions, its understanding of what it means to have God's Word in this world. Those who do not see this are out of touch with the deep realities of life, mistaking changes

on the surface for changes in the deep waters that flow beneath. An inspired group of marketers might find a way of reviving a flagging business by modifying its image and offerings, but the matters of the heart, the matters of God, are not susceptible to such cosmetic alteration. The world's business and God's business are two different things.[3]

Though I knew that last sentence is true, I spent many Sunday nights tossing and turning because attendance, offerings, or new memberships were down. It was an illusion that was hard to shake, and it made the threat of not being a "successful" minister one of the enemies who showed up nearly every morning outside my window.

Conflict and the Illusion of Having to Please People

Propping up that ever-present fourth enemy—having to deal with conflict in the church—was an illusion closely aligned with the first illusion to meet people's expectations. It was the illusion that *the role of Christian ministers is to please people.* Once again, my head recognized that illusion for exactly what it was: completely misguided thinking about my role as a pastor. But my heart never quite got the message, and I spent my entire ministry wanting to be universally loved and lauded.

I once served on an ordination committee at our church. We were charged with the task of determining whether or not a young man in our church should be ordained as a minister of the gospel. I didn't know Charles well, but, in my few dealings with him, had found him to be bright, personable, and passionate about serving God as a pastor. I assumed our committee would interview him a few times and unanimously recommend to the church that we ordain him.

But it didn't go quite that smoothly. Some on the committee, who knew Charles much better than I did, said that he had one fatal flaw of creating dissension and hard feelings everywhere he went. They said Charles would go out of his way to be contrary and that he loved to argue. Red flags suddenly started waving in my brain. If there is one thing a modern pastor cannot be, it is someone who is an expert at creating dissension and starting arguments. I started having misgivings about ordaining Charles as a minister.

But for every Charles who tends to antagonize people, there are probably ten ministers who go out of their way to placate and please people. I have observed that most ministers are "pleasers" who will bend over backwards to make people happy. We crave harmony and peace, and we wonder why the church is so full of angry people stirring up trouble. Why can't people just get along? Why can't we all just love the Lord and one another? And why can't people see that I'm a real prince of a pastor who deserves to be universally loved and lauded?

My wish to be universally loved and lauded as a pastor may have come from my parents or my past, but it most assuredly did not come from the Bible. Based on biblical evidence alone, no minister would expect to be liked by everyone—even everyone in the church.

Jesus, our Lord and Savior and number one role model, ended up being crucified on a cross between two thieves. And the apostle Paul, another of our heroes of faith, was anything *but* loved and lauded. He was whipped, imprisoned, chased out of towns, and branded a lunatic. Based on those two examples alone, one would have to conclude that Christian ministry is for people with thick skin and tenacious commitment. If the experience of Jesus and Paul are any kind of guide, Christian ministry is for people who can endure both hardship and hatred. As I said earlier, ministry is not for wimps.

I have even wondered how the apostle Paul would fare in the modern church. My guess is that he would be a colossal flop. His interpersonal skills were lacking. He knew nothing, evidently, about public relations. He missed the class on how to be subtle and tactful. And he, like Charles, seemed more argumentative and outspoken than he needed to be.

If a modern church would hire Paul as its pastor—which I doubt—he probably wouldn't last long. People would say he was too headstrong and passionate, that contemporary believers don't like the kind of fanaticism Paul espouses. And they would say he needs a personality overhaul—more humor, more stories in his sermons, more open-mindedness, less browbeating, less doctrine, and less intensity. I'm afraid someone like Paul would have a short shelf life in the contemporary church.

But, for all his flaws, let's give Paul his due. He was tough as a boot. He was more concerned about character than personality. And he wasn't about to cater to the crowd, because he had his eyes resolutely riveted on Christ. Paul serves as a fine corrective to those of us who worship at the idol of unanimous approval. He reminds us that there are more important things than popularity, that the approval of Christ trumps the approval of the crowd, and that having to deal with conflict is part and parcel of ministry.

Maybe all of us who minister in the name of Jesus need a few enemies and occasional conflict so that we never become *WIMPS (Witnesses Interested in Mostly People Skills)*. Once we come to grips with the fact that someone somewhere might not like us, we can then come to grips with the fact that conflict is an inevitable, and sometimes even healthy, part of life in any church.

Easier said than done, though, I must add.

Too Many Hats and the Illusion of Perfection

The fifth enemy that snarled at me most mornings—all of the daunting hats I had to wear as a minister—received impetus and energy from the illusion that *I have to succeed at everything I try.* The first illusion I discussed was about our need to meet others' expectations; this fifth one is the need we have to meet our own expectations.

I mentioned in the last chapter that of the eleven hats I had to wear as a pastor, I was mediocre or lousy at seven of them. Though I knew that and admitted it to myself, I was a bit more reluctant to admit it to our church's personnel committee that reviewed me every year. The public admission of flaws and shortcomings is best reserved for retirement.

But every minister has flaws and shortcomings that are the source of much stress in ministry. We have all of these hats we have to wear, but we can wear only a few of them well. So what do we do with the rest of them? Well, we put them on and do our best. We ask God to help us improve. We hope against hope that our church will be gracious to us. And, over time, we learn to be gracious to ourselves.

It is not appointed to one minister to be an expert in all things ministerial, so we learn to accentuate our strengths and improve our weaknesses.

When I try to evaluate how proficiently I wore the eleven hats of ministry, I would grade myself like this (on a scale of Good, Average, or Lousy):

• *Preacher—Good.* I liked to preach, enjoyed sermon preparation, and spent a lot of time each week getting ready to deliver the Word. This was one hat I really liked to wear and felt comfortable wearing.

• *Caregiver—Good.* The older I got, the more I liked pastoral care. Early in my ministry, I didn't particularly like hospital or nursing home visitation, but later in my ministry, I looked forward to visiting people who were sick, lonely, or simply in need of a personal call. When I was doing pastoral care, I felt that I was doing something tangible and personal to make a difference in someone's life.

• *Friend—Good.* I liked meeting people for lunch, attending kids' ballgames, sipping coffee with people who stopped by the church, talking sports over church supper on Wednesday nights, and getting to know people in a personal way. I look back now on many friends who connected with me over my years of ministry.

• *Counselor—Average.* I was an average counselor, I think, though I did appreciate the opportunity of walking with people through hard times. I was always better at feeling alongside people and identifying with their problems than I was at knowing how to solve them.

• *Business Executive—Lousy.* I always dreaded "institutional stuff"—budget planning, building programs, committee meetings, bylaw revisions, and long-range planning sessions. My last church, sensing my dislike of such things (and my inadequacies in attending to them), wisely hired an associate pastor to serve as "business administrator."

• *Visionary—Lousy.* Though it hurts me to admit it, I was a lousy visionary. I was more of a plodder. I could put my hand to the plow and never look back, but I wasn't adept at dreaming new dreams and seeing new visions. I was mostly content with the church the way it was and never felt a great compulsion to change it. Those who wanted me to think "outside the box," were, no doubt, disappointed.

• *Boss—Average.* I think I was an average boss to our staff because I liked them so much as people. I enjoyed my fellow staff members as friends. I wasn't good at supervision, though, and absolutely horrible at any kind of discipline. My tendency was to hire good, competent people and leave them alone.

• *Scholar—Average.* I was an average scholar because I read constantly. But a Greek or Hebrew scholar I was not. I tended to avoid the theoretical and doctrinal in my preaching and focused on the simple and practical essentials of discipleship. Very few listeners ever complained that my sermons were "over their head."

• *Evangelist—Lousy.* I was a lousy evangelist if you measure evangelism in typical ways. I didn't knock on doors, speak to strangers on airplanes, hand out tracts, or have our church sing twelve verses of an invitation hymn. I hope, in quiet ways and through reflective sermons, that I was able to point people toward Christ. By modern, measurable standards, though, I didn't wear this hat well— or comfortably.

• *Public Relations Expert—Lousy.* I dreaded being the "designated pray-er" at meetings, representing our church at associational or denominational functions, or having to play the role of holy person in secular gatherings. I often went out of my way to appear "normal" and not your typical "reverend." I'm afraid I flunked public relations for ministers.

• *Writer—Good.* I have always loved to write and looked forward to any chance I had to hurl words at paper. As I have confessed elsewhere, writing for me has been a "blissful affliction," and I've been addicted to it most of my life.

If one of my children had brought home such a report card, I would have been concerned that my child wasn't doing well at school. Four "Good's," three "Average's," and four "Lousy's" would have made me wonder if my child would even make it to the next grade. Face to face with that kind of report card, I would have known that my offspring was not an academic superstar. And, no doubt, I would have been disheartened and disillusioned by that realization.

Once we ministers discover we're not ministerial superstars, we will probably go through a time of disillusionment, too. But, thank God, it can be a blessed, productive disillusionment. Face to face with who we really are—flawed people with our fair share of short-comings—we can then relax into the joy of ministry. Yes, we're not perfect. Yes, we're lousy at some of the things we need to do. And, yes, we're fully aware of our imperfections. If, by chance, a disgruntled church member starts circulating a petition listing our flaws, we'll be the first to sign it.

For it is in seeing ourselves as we truly are that can lean into our strengths and improve our weaknesses. And it is in seeing ourselves as we truly are that can help us eventually love other people as *they* truly are.

Wreckage and the Illusion of Omniscience

Buttressing the sixth and final stress I mentioned in the last chapter— the pain of having to observe all the wreckage in the world—was the illusion that *I need to have the answers for all the world's problems.*

It's bad enough that we ministers have to walk among the wreckage caused by disease, divorce, depression, death, doubt, and all the other awful "D's." It's even worse, though, when we feel we have to be able to explain that wreckage or feel solely responsible for alleviating it.

People drowning in the mysteries and imponderables of life need someone to make sense of the senselessness of it all. And who better than their minister to have the right word, the perfect Bible verse, the correct counseling technique, the one prayer that really works, the right touch on the shoulder that brings comfort? Who better to explain and eliminate the pain of all that wreckage than you and me?

Again, we know better than to believe that. We know that we don't have all the answers and that we don't have any extraordinary power or expertise to solve problems. The problem is that many people in our church don't know that. They see us as having a special relation-ship with God that gives us extraordinary power and expertise. In an understandable desire not to burst their bubble and reveal how ordinary we really are, we play the game of "the wise minister." We put a wise expression on our face, adopt a wise tone of voice, and speak wise words of counsel. We might not have extraordinary power or expertise, but we would rather the church think otherwise.

Is there any character in literature more anxiety ridden than the poor wizard of Oz? He's just an ordinary fellow—"just a humbug," he finally confesses—but everyone thinks he's a wizard, and he feels he has to live up to their expectations. So he stays hidden, pretending to be something he's not so he can keep up appearances and maintain his image.

How many of us who minister in the name of Christ are just like that? People assume we're the wizard, with some kind of God-given wisdom and power that they don't have. And, though we know that is not true, we have appearances to keep and expectations to meet. So we play the game, try our best to act "wizardly," and hope no one learns the truth.

But there is a lot of stress in playing the role of a wizard. Eventually, playing that role takes its toll on the life of a minister. It would be much better for all concerned if someone would do for the minister what Toto did for the wizard—call his hand and reveal to everyone who he really is. Then the minister could quit pretending and be real. And once he does that, the Scarecrow might be able to get his brain, the Tin Woodsman his heart, and the Cowardly Lion his courage. Once the minister gets real, others might take the cue and do the same.

I don't think there is one thing we can do about all the wreckage in our ministries. People will continue to experience unfathomable pain, and we will continue to walk beside them when they do. But there *is* something we can do about the illusion of having all the answers and dispensing all the solutions. We can come out from behind the curtain. We can be real, honest, perplexed human beings. And, in our authenticity, we can call forth the best in the Scarecrows, Tin Woodsmen, and Cowardly Lions around us.

The Truth Will Set You Free

Jesus once said, "Then you will know the truth, and the truth will set you free" (John 8:32). That verse applies not only to seekers trying to find a philosophy by which to live but also to ministers trying to get rid of harmful illusions. The more illusions we can dispel and the more truth we can embrace in our lives and ministries, the more we will be set free. And the more we will be able to set others free.

The six enemies and stresses I mentioned in the last chapter get their power from the six illusions I just delineated. The stresses are the fruit, but the illusions are the root. Underneath these stresses that greeted me daily when I was a pastor were the dastardly root illusions that fed and nourished them. If I could have gotten rid of the illusions, the stresses would have melted away.

But getting rid of illusions is no easy task. As I have said repeatedly, we know in our head that these are illusions. Or, at least, I did. I knew that I couldn't meet the expectations of everyone in my church. I knew I wasn't the only Bible people would read. I knew that bigger is not always better. I knew that my ministry involved more than pleasing people. I knew I couldn't possibly succeed at wearing all the hats I needed to wear. And I knew I wasn't omniscient, that I didn't have answers for all the wreckage around me. But *knowing* something and *feeling* something are two very different things. As we preachers are prone to say, it's a long journey from the head to the heart.

Many mornings, when I gazed out the window and tried to ascertain which enemies were encircling my camp that day, my heart took over. Those illusions rose up, made small enemies into sinister monsters, and sent me to the church in fear and trembling.

May your vision be clearer than mine. May what you know in your head settle into your heart. May you get rid of those illusions as fast as you can, so the enemies won't linger and get stronger as the days go by.

Ministers who, like the Preacher in Ecclesiastes, lose their illusions have the best hope of finding a ministry that enriches both their own lives and the lives of those to whom they minister. And those ministers who become blessedly disillusioned are also the ones who are able to look out the window in the morning and see the amazing horses and chariots of fire that have come to their aid.

Notes

1. Karl Olsson, *Come to the Party* (Waco: Word Books, 1972) 30.

2. Ibid., 162.

3. David Wells, *God in the Wasteland* (Grand Rapids MI: Eerdmans, 1994) 30.

Chapter 4

Longing for Tarshish: Ministering in the Midst of the Ordinary

When you read the book of Jonah, it's hard to tell if Jonah was running away from God or Nineveh, the place to which God had called him. Certainly, Nineveh was no "destination place" for a prophet wanting to climb the ladder of ministerial success. Nineveh was known for its evil, its bad reputation, and its failed history. It would not have been a feather in anyone's cap to be the pastor of First Church, Nineveh.

So when the call came to go to Nineveh, Jonah got up and went—only he headed for Tarshish, not Nineveh. Jonah was more than willing to get up and go; he just wanted to specify exactly where he was going. And Tarshish was much more exotic than Nineveh. It was a place of intrigue and fascination. In 1 Kings 10:22, we read that ships from King Solomon's fleet went to Tarshish and returned with gold, silver, ivory, monkeys, and peacocks. Now you're talking! I don't know about you, but that's the kind of place I want to be. If there's an opening at First Church, Tarshish, would you put my name in the hat?

But we know all too well the rest of the Jonah story. The storm. The giant fish. The prayer from the belly of that fish. And the eventual journey to where God wanted him to be: "And Jonah got up and went to Nineveh, according to the LORD's word" (Jonah 3:3). Once

Jonah got to Nineveh, it was as bad as he thought it would be. He became angry and depressed, and, when the curtain closes at the end of the Jonah story, he is still angry and depressed.

We wish the story had a happier ending—that Jonah found great satisfaction in his ministry in Nineveh and thanked God for not sending him to Tarshish—but that's not the way it goes. The story leaves us with a disgruntled prophet, perhaps still harboring dreams of Tarshish and ruing the day he ever landed in Nineveh.

Ministering in Nineveh

Perhaps you can relate to Jonah. I certainly could when I was a pastor. There were many days when I wished I was anywhere but where I was—ministering among those petty, bickering, sinful people in Nineveh. I wanted to be where there was gold, silver, ivory, monkeys, and peacocks. I needed something more exciting and stimulating. The thought of the next church council meeting or potluck supper no longer charged my battery.

That's why I underscored in bold yellow ink the following passage from Eugene Peterson's book *Under the Unpredictable Plant*:

> If I succeed in getting anyone's attention, what I want to say is that the pastoral vocation is not a glamorous vocation and that Tarshish is a lie. Pastoral work consists of modest, daily, assigned work. Most pastoral work involves routines similar to cleaning out the barn, mucking out the stalls, spreading manure, pulling weeds. This is not, any of it, bad work in itself, but if we expected to ride a glistening black stallion in daily parades and then return to the barn where the lackey grooms our steed for us, we will be severely disappointed and end up being horribly resentful.[1]

Once we accept the fact that we have signed up to clean out the barn, muck out the stalls, spread the manure, and pull the weeds, we are well on our way to understanding our calling. Some ministers might get to ride those black stallions, but most of us don't. We get to minister in Nineveh, the less-than-exotic place where God has called us.

Our ministry in Nineveh involves *ordinary actions* for *ordinary people* in an *ordinary place*. That's the best definition of Christian ministry I've been able to come up with. It might not be a particularly exciting definition, but it *is* honest, and it does describe how most of us who minister spend our days.

We do *ordinary actions*. Yes, some of us get to mount the pulpit and preach the word of the Lord. Perhaps some of us even get to speak at conferences, attend our book signings, or do something else that is both public and glamorous. But, most of the time, our ministry takes place in ordinary ways. We stop by the nursing home to see Mrs. Thompson. We attend a child's tee-ball game. We listen to a hurting staff member at the office coffee pot. We take a grieving church member to lunch. None of those things will ever make headlines, but, without them, our ministry will be empty and ineffective. The best ministry we ever do will not be measured in numbers and will never be noticed by the masses.

We do ordinary actions for *ordinary people*. There were times, when I was a pastor, that I was initially intimidated by someone in our church. The author of those erudite books. The PhD who taught at the university. The lawyer who won all of those high-powered trials. They seemed so extraordinary—until I got to know them and learned how ordinary they really were. It turns out the author was lonely and needed a friend, the PhD knew nothing about the Bible, and the lawyer was burned out and wanted to quit his practice and start making handcrafted furniture. Who knew these people I had put on pedestals were as hurt, hungry, and haunted as the rest of us? Stare at anyone perched atop a pedestal long enough and that person will come toppling down.

Peterson goes on to say,

On close examination, though, it turns out that there are no wonderful congregations. Hang around long enough and sure enough there are gossips who won't shut up, furnaces that malfunction, sermons that misfire, disciples who quit, choirs that go flat—and worse. Every congregation is a congregation of sinners. As if that weren't bad enough, they all have sinners for pastors.[2]

For better or worse, that's the way it is in our churches. The people around us—especially as we really get to know them—are flawed, ordinary, and sinful. We might have thought, or wished, we were ministers to the superstars, but we quickly learned the truth. We're ordinary ministers trying to build the kingdom of God with ordinary people.

We do ordinary actions for ordinary people in an *ordinary place.* When Sherry and I travel around Texas, I have a line I use a lot when we go through some dusty town out in the middle of nowhere. I jokingly say, as we pass a clapboard church on the side of the road, "You could die on the vine right there at First Church, Podunk, Texas." But it's true. You *could* die on the vine right there. There's no Starbucks, no bookstore, no theater, no supermarket in Podunk. It would be easy to wither and die right there.

But Podunk needs the gospel. And Podunk needs a minister who will come and invest her life there. Yes, you could die on the vine there, but you could also *find* life there and be a source of life for others. You could fashion a life there that has meaning and joy in it. The challenges in Podunk are at least as great as the challenges in Chicago or New York.

Let's just acknowledge that staying alive in Podunk, and conveying the good news in Podunk, is enough to keep any minister occupied for a long while. But trying to bring life and love to Podunk is a calling that many ministers would run from—the way Jonah ran from Nineveh.

Ordinary actions for *ordinary people* in an *ordinary place.* That's our calling and our job description. Peterson is right: Tarshish is a lie. We are smack-dab in the middle of Nineveh, and we might as well admit and embrace it.

The challenge any minister faces, in light of that calling and job description, is staying alive and enthused in the face of such "ordinariness." What we ministers do most of the time seems so ordinary and uneventful. The people to whom we minister seem ordinary, too. And the place we minister—whether Podunk or downtown Los Angeles—eventually seems ordinary as well. Put your hand to any plow long enough, and you will eventually become tired and discouraged by the sameness of it all.

In his book *Freedom for Ministry*, Richard John Neuhaus warns of the monotony inherent in the ministerial calling. On one of those long afternoons when I couldn't hear the sound of trumpets, I marked this passage in the book and referred back to it on several occasions:

> As with the children of Israel in the wilderness, there are dry and difficult times in ministry. There are stale periods when mystical vision is smothered, prophecy seems pretentious, and even the apocalyptic sounds prosaic. One learns not to panic at the appearance of monotony. But neither should one be casual about the rot that can set in and finally rob ministry of its joy and venture. For very few people is life lived consistently on the felt edge of new discovery. Most of us know and expect the feeling that we are meeting events and ourselves coming around again in all too predictable a fashion.
>
> As preachers, for instance, we are properly depressed to hear ourselves repeating ourselves. The answer is not to feign excitement about exhausted ideas and emotions. There are few things so distasteful or so unpersuasive as forced enthusiasm. The better answer is to be prepared for such periods of weariness and to respond to them with a disciplined program of prayer, study, and hard thought.[3]

Neuhaus offers two warnings in that paragraph that can help us as we deal with boring, tedious life in our Nineveh. First, he warns us "not to panic at the appearance of monotony." One response to the tedium of Nineveh is to panic and decide to hit the road, to try to find a place more exotic than where we are. We can all too easily have a knee-jerk reaction to the humdrum of Nineveh and assume that God must surely be calling us elsewhere—preferably, of course, to some place like Tarshish.

But, second, Neuhaus warns us "not to be casual about the rot that can set in and finally rob ministry of its joy and venture." The other response is to sit in Nineveh forever—bored, unfulfilled, and ineffective. Being faithful to God is not synonymous with "dying on the vine," and it is not particularly virtuous to do nothing while the rot does its dastardly work on our spirit. Being too quick to leave Nineveh is not a good option, but neither is dying of misery and boredom there.

It's worth probing those two responses a little deeper, I think, so that we can avoid them both. If we ministers can learn how not to panic and how not to rot, perhaps we can learn how to stay alive and be effective right where we are.

Not to Panic

A couple of years ago, Sherry and I put our names on a long waiting list to get a community garden plot. We got word about a month ago that one had finally become available, so we became the proud owners, or at least renters, of a ten-by-ten plot of land at Milburn Park about a mile from our house. We're full-fledged farmers now, sowing and (we hope) reaping in our little garden plot.

Anyone who has ever done any farming or gardening discovers what we are now experiencing: tending a garden involves a lot of dull, monotonous work. Our little plot wasn't in very good shape, so we had to hoe and pull weeds several times to get it ready to plant. Then we had to buy compost and peat moss to put in our garden to enrich the soil. Next, we had to buy seeds and plant them. Now we have to go to our plot every other day to water it and keep the weeds at bay.

It's still fun for us because "the new has not yet worn off," but check with me in a few months, and I'll let you know how we're feeling then. Once the weather turns hot, the bugs show up, and our plants don't produce the bountiful crop of vegetables we're envisioning, I might be singing a different tune. It's entirely possible that our trips to the garden plot will become dreaded obligations, not exciting adventures.

I think my gardening experience is an apt metaphor for ministry. When I began my work as pastor of a church, I was always filled with excitement. Who knew what exciting things were ahead of us? Who knew how many people we would touch with the good news of the gospel? Who knew how many new friends we would make and how many new ministries we would start? I went to work every morning excited even about mundane things like staff meetings and budget preparation.

But, inevitably, the new wore off. Reality eventually set in, and I found myself doing very ordinary things with very ordinary people in a very ordinary place. When I first arrived at the church, I heard trumpets every morning, but somewhere along the way, the trumpets got muffled by tedium. What I was doing most days seemed insignificant. The people in the church had shown themselves to be not nearly as sharp and committed as I thought they were. And, though the church was located near a thriving city, we were stuck out in the suburbs where the most exciting thing to do was shop at the local mall.

When we find ourselves in such a moment, on that day when the new has officially worn off, what shall we do? Well, what we shall *not* do is panic and bolt for Tarshish. What we should do, I think, is recognize the work to which we have been called and affirm that it is neither glamorous nor exotic. What we should do is keep hoeing, keep planting, keep watering, and keep trusting that God will use our efforts to produce a crop.

Actually, I'm not the first one to recognize the similarities between farming and ministering. In his book *The Contemplative Pastor*, Eugene Peterson writes about poet/novelist/essayist Wendell Berry, whose works consistently espouse love and stewardship of the land:

> I enjoy reading the poet-farmer Wendell Berry. He takes a small piece of land in Kentucky, respects it, cares for it, submits himself to it just as an artist submits himself to his materials. I read Berry, and every time he speaks of "farm" and "land," I insert "parish." As he talks about his farm, he talks about what I've tried to practice in my congregation, because one of the genius aspects of pastoral work is locality.
>
> The pastor's question is, "Who are these particular people, and how can I be with them?" My job is simply to be there, teaching, preaching Scripture as well as I can, and being honest with them, not doing anything to interfere with what the Spirit is shaping in them. Could God be doing something that I never thought of? Am

I willing to be quiet for a day, a week, a year? Like Wendell Berry, am I willing to spend fifty years reclaiming this land? With these people?[4]

When Sherry and I head out, hoe in hand, to tend to plot sixteen at Milburn Park, I am doing what I did all those years I was a pastor. I will water, weed, fertilize, and wait patiently but expectantly for a crop. The stakes are not as high now at plot sixteen in Milburn Park as they were when I was doing those things as pastor at Andice, the Texas Baptist Children's Home, Heritage Park, and Woodland, but the tasks are basically the same.

Recently, when we made our journey to plot sixteen, we were shocked to see that some of our newly rooted plants had been devoured by something or someone. One of our fellow gardeners told us that a rabbit regularly visits the community garden plot to enjoy his own version of a potluck supper. Evidently, plot sixteen was one of his stops.

What should we do in such a situation? Throw up our hands and quit the gardening business? Grow depressed and discouraged about our chances of growing a good garden? Start stalking the garden at night hoping to catch that dastardly rabbit? No, what we shall do is tend those damaged plants, try to bring them back to health, and then renew our efforts to produce a good crop. We refuse to panic because of one nocturnal rabbit; in fact, we couldn't really call ourselves gardeners if we despaired over such a small incident.

Those of us who minister in any kind of spiritual garden will encounter numerous such rabbits. There will be nasty people, unpleasant situations, and more conflict than we care to encounter. But we know that ministry is for people who will put their hands to the plow and keep plowing. We will not panic the first time—or the hundredth time—that we experience a problem.

We will not book passage to Tarshish the first time things get hard or humdrum in Nineveh.

Not to Rot

While it is true that we ministers cannot panic at the first sign of tedium or trouble and head for Tarshish, it is also true that we cannot sit idly by while spiritual rot eats away at our spirits. Not panicking in Nineveh is a good idea, but so is not sinking into the slough of despondency.

I think that every minister has to come up with a personal plan for surviving in Nineveh. There's not a one-size-fits-all plan for ministerial survival, and each of us has to fashion one that fits *us* and keeps *us* alive. I never wrote down a plan for my survival as a pastor, but, as I reflect on my ministry now, I realize that I did have one. It was not particularly exciting or creative, but I suppose it fit me and fed my spirit. Say what you might about the ordinariness of my strategy for surviving the rigors of ministry, but it got me to the finish line in reasonably good shape.

My strategy for "hanging in there" in Nineveh included several key ingredients:

People. My Uncle Glen was not the only person who was willing to sit with me under the juniper tree. I had other friends, both inside the church and out, with whom I could be honest and bare my soul. These folks were both available and authentic, which made them ideal "ministry savers."

I also always had outside groups that had nothing to do with the church and thus provided me some needed breathing room. I always had a tennis group—some guys who were more interested in my backhand than in my theology. And a barbecue group—people who would meet me at one of our favorite barbecue places to feast on brisket and ribs. And a kids' sports group—parents of our kids' teammates, who shared with us a passion for sports, booster clubs, and the outcome of the next big game.

The blessing of these groups was that they gave me a life away from the church. When I stepped into these groups, I didn't have to be religious, "pastoral," or in charge; I just had to be a friend.

Places. At every church I served as pastor, I found sacred places— hiding places might be more honest—where we could go to escape the pressures of church life. Sherry's parents had a lake house in Trinity, Texas, that became our haven for years. Later, we discovered Port Aransas and fled to a beach-front condo there every chance we got. Then we found a quiet cabin in Ruidoso, New Mexico, that we nestled into every October for years. Late in my ministry, we started going to Alsea, Oregon, for a month every summer to escape the Texas heat and renew our souls.

Just writing about these places makes me a bit misty-eyed. They truly were holy places for us, and we are grateful both for those places and for the people who made them available to us. Inevitably, I would return from those places refreshed and better able to face whatever Nineveh wanted to throw at me.

Books. I am a confessed "bookaholic" and have bought and read thousands of books through the years. Books have not only been a source of entertainment and inspiration for me, though; I think they literally kept me alive on those days when I was under the juniper tree.

Where would I have been without Robert Capon, Frederick Buechner, Eugene Peterson, Karl Olsson, Barbara Brown Taylor, E. B. White, Wendell Berry, Rick Bass, George Sheehan, William Tapply, Louise Penny, and a host of other writers too numerous to mention? I'll tell you where I think I would have been—either stuck permanently under some juniper tree or failing miserably as a book-store owner in Galveston or Bandera. Books saved my ministry and also taught me the importance of fashioning sensible, compelling sentences.

Thursdays. I always took Thursday off and guarded that day carefully. On Thursday, I did nothing "churchy" if I could help it. Thursday was reserved for time with Sherry, breakfast at Denny's, a trip to the bookstore, or a quick trip to the beach. Thursday was for tennis with the "old tennis guys," working in the yard, or going to get ice cream at Baskin-Robbins.

In short, on Thursdays I was not a pastor; I was a person. And I'm convinced that I would not have survived in Nineveh without this one day each week to get away from the rigors and expectations of church life. I will always have a soft spot in my heart for Thursday.

Even though I'm now retired, I still consider it the best day of the week.

Anchors. It is easy to rot in Nineveh without theological anchors. Those of us who minister in the name of Christ desperately need a few essential truths that define us both as ministers and as human beings. Without these foundational anchors, we will be subject to the torpor that comes to any person who has lost his identity and floats aimlessly on the waters of life.

I will have more to say about this in the next chapter, but let's admit here that if we don't have a few core convictions that put a foundation under our ministry, we are destined to be sad examples of Jesus' story about the house built on the sand. The rain will fall, the floods will come, and the wind will blow and beat against our house. And the house will collapse and be completely destroyed because it had a flimsy foundation.

But once we get some crucial linchpins in place, the storms can blow all they want, and we will stand firm. Anchored by some key truths about God and ministry, we can be confident in who God is, who we are, and what we are called to be and do. Anyone marching to a divine drumbeat is not easily deterred by the world, or even by the church. And anyone who hears just the faint bleat of a bugle in the afternoon will have his or her spirit renewed.

Looking back on my ministry now, I think those were the five ingredients that kept me from sinking into rot and despair. Having some people who breathed life into my tired spirit, some places that gave me different sights to see and air to breathe, some books that allowed me to live in a different world for a while, one day every week when I could do fun things and restore my sanity, and some convictions about my role as a pastor that kept me focused all combined to get me to the finish line with my health and my faith intact.

Please don't feel obligated to adopt such a strategy yourself, but do give some thought to ways you can stay alive and not "die on the vine" in your Nineveh.

The Depressing Sound of Your Own Voice

So far, we have taken aim primarily at Nineveh and pinpointed it as the problem. Nineveh is ordinary. Nineveh lacks the intrigue of Tarshish. Nineveh offers us little in the way of new experiences and new discoveries. No doubt, those things are at least partially true, and we need to acknowledge them and deal with them.

But there is another factor that eventually becomes all too evident: *We* are pretty ordinary ourselves, and *we* have grown weary of the sound of our own very ordinary voices. The problem of ordinariness is not just "out there" in our church and town; it is also "in here," in us and our approach to ministry.

As Neuhaus put it in the quote I used earlier, "For very few people is life lived consistently on the felt edge of new discovery." That, sadly, describes our plight as ministers. We do not live on the felt edge of new discovery; in fact, we think, say, and do the same things over and over again. We might like to throw stones at church people for being so ordinary and stuck in a rut, but they could justifiably throw those same stones at us. Many long-time Christians must leave church every Sunday wondering if they will ever hear a fresh word or new thought from their ministers. The "you're-so-ordinary-you're-boring-me-to-death" gate swings both ways.

But admitting that will do two fine things for our ministry. First, it will keep us from being haughty. Confessing our own humanity and owning up to our ordinariness gets us off the pedestal and down among the common folks where we belong. Acknowledging that we, too, are stuck in a rut and that we, too, hunger for new truth and a fresh experience of God gives us opportunity to walk a mile in the shoes of the people we serve. Truth to tell, ministers on pedestals don't make very good ministers.

Second, it will give us an opportunity to change. As long as the problem is the church, we ministers have to accept no blame whatsoever and can, in righteous indignation, book passage to Tarshish as quickly as possible. But if the problem is also in us, if we admit to being stuck in a rut and saying the same clichés Sunday after Sunday, then perhaps we can begin to find new ways to come alive. We can try to find new angles on old Scripture passages, new ways to teach the

Bible to children, new ways to reach young people with the gospel, new ways to meet the needs of people in retirement homes, and new ways to do church in a changing world.

Once we ministers admit we're stuck in a rut and sick and tired of doing things the way we've always done them, we've taken the first step toward newness. Disenchantment with ourselves and weariness at the sound of our own voices can be the prelude to renewal.

But if we're painfully honest, most of us will concede that the real issue is deeper than the ones I've just delineated, deeper than new strategies for reaching people and doing church. The deeper issue is our own spiritual condition. In our kind of world, where a "perfect storm" threatens to capsize our ministry and send us headlong into despair, we need to have some deep anchors in place just to survive. We need deep theological and vocational anchors to keep us from drifting into either complacency or catastrophe. In the next chapter, I want to probe the issue of vocational identity—who we are as ministers and what we are called to do. To do that, let's shift our focus from Jonah running from Nineveh to a shepherd boy named David trying in vain to wear the king's armor.

Notes

1. Eugene Peterson, *Under the Unpredictable Plant* (Grand Rapids MI: Eerdmans, 1992) 16.

2. Ibid., 17.

3. Richard John Neuhaus, *Freedom for Ministry* (San Francisco: HarperSanFrancisco, 1979) 199–200.

4. Eugene Peterson, *The Contemplative Pastor* (Dallas: Word Books, 1989) 11.

Chapter 5

WEARING THE KING'S ARMOR: RECLAIMING OUR IDENTITY

The story of David and Goliath is the stuff movies are made of. It's the ultimate story of a triumphant underdog, the kind of story we Americans love. Even films like *Miracle, Cool Runnings*, and *Hoosiers* pale alongside the tale of a meek shepherd boy taking on a fearsome giant and defeating him in resounding fashion. The story of David and Goliath in 1 Samuel 17 is a timeless reminder that little guys can beat big guys and that absolutely nothing is impossible. If David can whip Goliath, then we, too, can whip whatever fearsome giant we happen to be facing.

Tucked away in that story is a scene that can be a good "jumping-off point" for those of us in ministry who want to remember who we are and what we're called to do. It's the part of the story where David tries to wear Saul's armor. David has volunteered to take on the giant Philistine named Goliath, and no one in his right mind gives him a chance of coming out of that encounter alive. But at least he should enter the fray as prepared as possible. At least he should wear the best armor so he will not be defenseless when the giant squashes him.

Here's the way the writer of 1 Samuel tells this part of the story:

Then Saul dressed David in his own gear, putting a coat of armor on him and a bronze helmet on his head. David strapped his sword on over the armor, but he couldn't walk around well because he'd never tried it before. "I can't walk in this," David told Saul, "because I've never tried it before." So he took them off. He then grabbed his staff and chose five smooth stones from the streambed. He put them in the pocket of his shepherd's bag and with sling in hand went out to the Philistine. (17:38-40)

The rest, as they say, is history. The five smooth stones were more than enough. David didn't need the king's armor; in fact, he probably would have been killed had he tried to wear it. He just needed his sling and five smooth stones, and he could do exactly what he needed to do.

The point I want to underscore in this chapter is that our culture has dictated to us the kind of armor we need to wear as ministers. It has been suggested, or at least implied, that if we want to make it in the current world, we need certain skills, priorities, and gifts. The fearsome giants of secularism, materialism, atheism, post-modernism, and all the other "ism's" that are so prevalent in our world can be slain only by ministers who go into battle armed with the king's armor.

But some of us have tried on that armor, and it didn't fit at all. Like David, we found ourselves muttering, "I can't wear this." We might have even said, "If I have to wear this, I'll probably die." Certainly we knew that if we had to wear that armor, we would be miserable human beings playing a religious game that we really didn't want to play.

In *Working the Angles*, Eugene Peterson says he could take anyone with a high school degree, give that person six months of training, and produce a minister that any church in America would be proud to have on its staff. The curriculum would consist of the following courses:

- *Creative Plagiarism.* The student would be exposed to a variety of sermons and books from which he or she could borrow prodigiously. Their origins could be changed just enough to be unrecognizable and assure that the minister would be known for keen insight as well as a fine sense of humor.

- *Voice Control for Prayer and Counseling.* The student would be taught a "Holy Joe" tone of voice that would convey an unmistakable aura of sanctity and spirituality.
- *Efficient Office Management.* The student would be taught how to run a tight administrative ship, for nothing impresses a modern church more than efficiency.
- *Image Projection.* The student would learn half a dozen easily implemented devices for appearing to be an important and highly sought after spiritual leader.

After listing this tongue-in-cheek course of study, Peterson adds this postscript:

> I have been laughing for several years over this trade school training for pastors with which I plan to make my fortune. Recently, though, the joke has backfired on me. I keep seeing advertisements for institutes and workshops all over the country that invite pastors to sign up for this exact curriculum. The advertised course offerings are not quite as honestly labeled as mine, but the content appears to be identical—a curriculum that trains pastors to satisfy the consumer tastes in religion. I'm not laughing anymore.[1]

Anyone who is serious about ministry for Christ in the modern world is not laughing either. If that's the armor we're expected to wear, count us out. We know we need more than techniques, strategies, and PR expertise to be what we want to be and do what we're called to do.

I want to suggest an alternative to the curriculum Peterson jokingly outlined. I want to offer five smooth stones we can use to reclaim our identity—and maybe save our sanity in the process. The five stones I'm going to mention come from a familiar streambed: the life of Jesus. If we want to recover our identity as ministers, if we want to see our true job description, we need look no further than the story of Jesus, a story we already know so well. Embedded in that story is a view of ministry big enough and important enough to make us see what ministry *can* be and *ought* to be. In the story of Jesus, we can recover our identity and, perhaps, recover the wonder of our call.

Birth and the Power of Incarnation

The Gospel of John gives us no details about Jesus' birth, but it does give us this priceless pearl about the miracle of the incarnation: "The Word became flesh and made his home among us. We have seen his glory, glory like that of a father's only son, full of grace and truth" (Jn 1:14).

That verse spells out what the rest of the New Testament makes clear: to reach human beings and to communicate fully with them, God had to become a human being. As one preacher put it so poetically, "On Christmas morning, God walked down the stairs of heaven with a baby in his arms." God could not just shout divine instructions from the halls of heaven. God had to "walk down the stairs" and get mixed up in all the messy particulars of human life. To truly touch us, God had to become one of us.

Ever since John wrote that line in John 1, it has been a reminder to Jesus' followers that ministry is always supposed to be incarnational. In Jesus, the Word became flesh, and, ever since Jesus, his followers have had to *keep* making that Word flesh. Taking the original incarnation as our model, we have known that we can't shout words of advice and wisdom to people; we have to become mixed up in all the messy particulars of their lives.

I feel quite certain that the incarnation was the source of much misery and frustration for Jesus. He had to live, for example, in a community of friends who were hard-headed, power-hungry, and, in the end, shamefully timid. When the chips were down and Jesus needed men who would stand with him in his time of death, they all forsook him and fled.

It would have been so much easier for Jesus if he could have lobbed words of wisdom at them from a distance, sent them a book to read, or suggested that they enroll in a correspondence course in personal godliness. But he couldn't. He had to travel with them, laugh with them, cry with them, and, as John put it, make his home with them. Incarnational ministry is hands-on, intimate—and painful.

Those of us who have responded to God's call to ministry have taken on the task of trying to en-flesh the Word by making our home with ordinary folks. We sit by their bedside when they're sick, give them high-fives when their daughter hits a home run, laugh with them around the table at the Wednesday night supper, hold their hands when they stand beside the casket, and, in a thousand other ways, connect our lives with theirs.

As it was for Jesus, incarnational ministry for us is both rewarding and repugnant. It is rewarding because we get to connect with people at the most crucial moments in their lives. Many times, we ministers get to stand on holy ground with people, and, as a result, we do not lack for meaningful, God-filled experiences. Incarnational ministry is ministry at its best.

But incarnational ministry is also repugnant and frustrating. Getting mixed up with the messy particulars of human life puts us right where Jesus often was—dealing with sinful, misguided, angry people. We probably have our own version of Peter, James, and John—people wanting to be in positions of power and authority and wreaking havoc on group harmony. We probably have our own version of Judas, too—people who betray us and turn their backs on us. Certainly, we have our own version of the disciples as a group— people who don't understand who we are as ministers and keep trying to pull us in another direction.

Notice how often the Gospel writers mention that Jesus went off by himself. Maybe that was so he could be with God, but maybe it was because he couldn't stand his disciples anymore. I often said that being a pastor would be the best job in the world—if it weren't for the people!

Jesus endured that incarnational agony, I think, because he knew that was the only way to communicate what he was called to communicate. As frustrating as it was to walk with those misguided disciples, Jesus knew it was the only way to convey the good news of his kingdom. If they were going to "get it," it would be because they "caught it" from him. The Word had to become flesh if they were ever going to see his glory.

But they eventually did see his glory. And it's interesting to notice how John describes that glory. He doesn't describe Jesus' glory in terms of cherubim and seraphim or anything miraculous; he describes it in terms of grace and truth. Jesus, he says, was full of grace and truth.

Every day as they traveled with Jesus, the disciples got a crash course in grace. In the way he related to them. In the way he related to common sinners. In the way he welcomed children and women. In the way he dealt with conflict. In the way he faced his own death. Jesus was full of grace, and the only way the disciples would learn to live with grace themselves was to walk every day by his side. They got to see grace in action, which was better than any sermon Jesus could have preached.

They also got to see truth in action. Jesus not only lived with grace; he lived with truth. Every day those disciples got to see truth both proclaimed and practiced. They were able to hear and see the truth about God, themselves, the kingdom Jesus came to establish, and the way they were supposed to relate to the people around them. John would later write in his Gospel these words of Jesus: "You will know the truth, and the truth will set you free" (Jn 8:32). As Jesus walked and talked with them, the disciples gradually learned the truth that would set them free.

That's why Jesus "hung in there" through all the frustrations he experienced with his friends. He knew that he had to be one of them, walk with them, even suffer because of them if they were going to learn the way of grace and truth. If they were ever going to learn the way of true glory, it would be because they finally "caught it" from him.

Incarnational ministry in every generation understands that reality. The only way people in any generation learn the way of truth and grace is to catch it from someone who walks with them on a regular basis. The call to ministry in Jesus' day, and in our day, is to make the Word flesh so that people can see a better way, a way of glory, a way of grace and truth. Our calling as ministers today is to en-flesh grace and truth, to model it everywhere we go, and to pray that, in spite of our frequent failures and shortcomings, people will still be able to see "the glory" when we are among them.

Baptism and the Power of Blessing

When Jesus launched his public ministry, he was baptized by his cousin, John the Baptist. That baptism was marked by a miracle. As

Jesus came up out of the water, "A voice from heaven said, 'This is my Son whom I dearly love; I find happiness in him'" (Matt 3:17).

I can't help wondering how many times Jesus thought back to that experience to find encouragement and hope in his ministry. When his disciples were thick-headed and confused, when the religious authorities hounded him, when he traipsed from dusty town to dusty town trying to convey the good news, and when he faced the horrors of a cruel crucifixion, he must have "flashed back" to his baptism and remembered those glorious words. "This is my Son whom I dearly love. I find happiness in him." Those words can get a person through many an ordeal.

And they remind us of another stone we ministers must have in our pockets: the blessing of God on our lives so that we can be a blessing to others. Until we ourselves have the acceptance, freedom, forgiveness, and presence of God in our lives, how can we hope to be agents of blessing to unblessed people? How can anyone "catch" from us something we don't have?

Jacob's story in Genesis 32 is a story that must be repeated in our lives. Jacob wrestled with a mysterious stranger whom he at least knew was a representative of God. The two wrestled through the night until the divine stranger said, "Let me go because the dawn is breaking." Jacob responded, "I won't let you go until you bless me" (Gen 32:26). We must wrestle with God—all night if necessary—until we get that blessing.

Early in my first pastorate, I read the book I've already quoted a couple of times, *Come to the Party*, which changed both my life and my ministry. It enabled me to see the necessity of receiving God's blessing—and how much I had hungered for that blessing all my life.

I grew up with what I would call an "offering envelope approach to God." I was raised in a strict Baptist church, filled with kind and devoted people. Every year, our church gave each of us a stack of offering envelopes. Obviously, those envelopes were primarily given to encourage us to make a weekly gift to the church. But they also bore a checklist of religious activities we were supposed to do, and, if we did them, we got to put a check in the boxes on the envelope.

We got to check a box if we brought an offering, stayed for worship, did our daily Bible readings, studied our Sunday school lesson, or were on time for Sunday school. Anyone who could check all the boxes on the offering envelope could write a big "100" in the final box. My goal, every week, was to be a 100 percent Christian.

There was nothing wrong with this at all, and I know that our offering envelopes were supposed to be tools that taught us important Christian disciplines. But the envelopes made a sensitive, people-pleasing boy like me believe that being a 100 percent Christian depended entirely on my personal performance. I came to believe that God would be disappointed in me if I couldn't check all the boxes—which is another way of saying that I became one of the "unblessed," one destined to struggle to earn God's acceptance.

I think the reason *Come to the Party* resonated so strongly with me is because its author, Karl Olsson, had a similar background. Here's the way he describes his spiritual struggle:

> I know a great deal about the unblessed minister, for I am one myself. I feel that I got my father's love but not his favor. All my life I have stayed at home in the father's house, devoting myself to religious interests of one kind or another. I have been a pastor, a chaplain, a teacher and administrator in a Christian college and seminary. The five years I spent in teaching and administration on a university campus were confusing for me because I didn't feel that I belonged. I felt disloyal to the church and to the Christian enterprise, which had claimed my loyalty.
>
> When I examine this vocational pattern more closely, I become convinced that my whole life has been devoted to a search for the blessing which I could never secure. I was one with the elder brother, convinced with him that if I did my homework and the chores, learned to tie the right knots and earn the right merit badges, and if I didn't carouse around and waste my substance but deposited my paychecks, one day I would make it and have the calf, the candles, and the party.[2]

Like me, Karl Olsson grew up trying to check all the boxes. But that approach to God leads to nothing but frustration and disillusionment.

No matter how good we are and how many boxes we check, we never feel satisfied. The calf, candles, and party remain somehow beyond our reach.

But Olsson finally had his Jacob-at-Peniel experience. He finally heard the message he had preached all his life—that we are justified by faith alone and not by works, that we are held in the gracious arms of One who loves us even if we don't check all the boxes. He realized that he could not do one religious thing to earn God's love, that he already had all the love God could give him. In short, Olsson finally let grace move from his head to his heart, and *Come to the Party* is his hymn of gratitude.

Once grace becomes something we experience and not just something we preach, we are free to be ourselves and to be human. And once that happens in us, we become agents of blessing to others. It's not like we have to run around looking for people to bless. People are not particularly clamoring to be objects of our ministry. But once we have the blessing, we can just be ourselves. As we move among people, we bless them without even being aware of it. Blessed people inevitably become agents of blessing to others.

That's why the message Jesus heard at his baptism is one we need to both know and preach. But, more to the point, we need to have our own baptism kind of experience, where we hear God say, "This is my son/daughter whom I love. I find happiness in him/her." That message will be especially crucial to us if we ever find ourselves under a juniper tree.

Teaching and the Power of the Word

After his baptism, Jesus launched a ministry of teaching. He moved from town to town telling delightful stories and announcing the arrival of the kingdom of God. And his teaching was unlike anything the people of his day had heard. Matthew comments, "When Jesus finished these words [what we know as the Sermon on the Mount], the crowds were amazed at his teaching because he was teaching them like someone with authority and not like their legal experts" (Matt 7:28-29). Jesus took words, crafted them into works of art, and captured the attention of common people.

Those of us who follow him try our best to do the same. Words are important to us. They are, in fact, the tools of our trade. Mark Twain once said that the difference between the right word and the almost right word is the difference between lightning and a lightning bug. Those of us who follow the Master Teacher always strive to find the right word so that lightning can flash in our teaching and preaching.

M. Craig Barnes has written a fine book suggesting that pastors start seeing themselves as poets. In *The Pastor as Minor Poet*, he describes how crucial this is for pastoral identity:

> When poetry dries up for pastors, they get as lost as their parishioners. It is then that they stop praying and give up expecting much to happen through their preaching or the tender words they offer in pastoral care. No longer believing in their own words, they assume the role of ecclesiastical managers who simply meet expectations. Some coast through the rest of their ministries without ever mentioning a sonnet for the soul again. Their sermons and prayers are little more than strung-together platitudes, and their pastoral care becomes equally petty. Others find that they can no longer live with themselves as ecclesiastical con artists and slowly self-destruct in front of the congregation. Either way, it is deadly to the church. There is no life without poetry, and there is no parish poet once he or she has lost belief in the Word. Even if the parishioners are possessed by too much despair to believe, they at least need to believe that their poet believes.[3]

There is a deadly progression in this paragraph, and I fear it is a slippery slope that is all too easy to get on.

First, *the poetry dies.* We forget we are poets, called to fashion words with precision and style. We forget that *how* we teach and preach is as crucial as *what* we teach and preach.

Second, *once the poetry dies, we quit expecting anything to happen in our ministry.* When we no longer believe in the power of words, our words become empty and trite. We no longer believe in the awesome power of the spoken or written word to move and transform people.

Third, *once the poetry dies and we quit expecting anything to happen in our ministry, we resort to serving as ecclesiastical managers who simply meet expectations.* Ministry becomes the drab job of tending an institution and placating people.

Fourth, *we eventually self-destruct.* Stuck with doing things we're not excited about and charged with making an institution stay afloat, we start to wither on the vine. This is not what we are called to do. As Barnes says elsewhere in his book, "A good poet is hard to find, and nothing is more tragic than wasting one in a busy office."[4]

Fifth, *the church starts to die.* The self-destructing pastor can no longer bring life and energy to the church, so the church starts to wither, too. There is no life without poetry, and, if the church has no one to compose the poems and shape the words, it is destined to decay. What started out as the seemingly innocuous problem of a pastor forsaking a poetic call ends up being the poison that kills a church.

The way to keep that progression from ever getting started, of course, is for pastors (and other ministers) to embrace and take delight in their roles as poets. If we can just remember that words are crucial to who we are and what we do, and that we follow One who treasured words and spoke as one who had authority, we can recover both our calling and our joy.

Recovering our role as teacher, preacher, and poet might even save our ministry. Barnes writes,

> I understand the decision to stop being a pastor. I even applaud it. Pastors have higher callings in life than being a pastor, and foremost among them is glorifying God. If it's no longer possible to do that in the role of a priest, then it is time to go. But it's impossible not to wonder if there is another way. What if instead of working so hard at omnicompetence, pastors were free to work hard simply being better poets? And is it possible that the call to parish ministry can come not at the expense of our souls, but at their delight—the joy known only by those who can behold the mystery and truth at work just beneath the surface of all the belief and all the reality of parish life?[5]

Death and the Power of the Cross

After about three years of teaching and ministering to common people, Jesus was falsely accused of criminal activity, subjected to a mockery of a trial, and then crucified on a cross between two thieves at a place called Golgotha. His death reminds us of a fourth stone that defines who we are as ministers of the gospel, a stone that gives us both purpose and power. We get the privilege of announcing Jesus' death to the world—as well as the glorious implications that go with that death.

There might not be any passage in the Bible more applicable to our culture—and our ministry to that culture—than Paul's words in 1 Corinthians 1. In his opening words to the Corinthian Christians, Paul gives a perfect description of the world in which we now minister.

He begins by declaring the supremacy of the cross. He says that the cross is foolishness to the culture at large, but it is the power of God for those who understand its power. He says that the Jews are looking for signs and the Greeks are looking for wisdom, but he is going to preach to them about the cross.

And he knows that his message will not be well received. The Jews will think his message of the cross is scandalous and the Greeks will think it is foolishness, but he is going to preach it anyway. The good news about Jesus and his cross, Paul says, is God's power and God's wisdom. So he writes, "I had made up my mind not to think about anything while I was with you except Jesus Christ, and to preach him as crucified" (1 Cor 2:2).

Things haven't changed much in two thousand years, have they? We all still minister in Corinth. Modern people are still looking for signs and seeking wisdom, and the message of the cross still sounds both scandalous and foolish. If you want to keep people away from your church in droves, I can tell you one way to do it: post on the sign out front a sermon title that has the word "cross" in it. That will guarantee an empty house.

People would much rather hear a sermon about building a healthy self-image, establishing a happy family, or knowing the biblical principles for financial prosperity. At least those topics are modern and relevant. Anything with "cross" in it seems dated and religious. Any modern minister who vows, with Paul, "I made up my mind not to think about anything while I was with you except Jesus Christ, and to preach him as crucified" will likely be branded "stodgy," "old-fashioned," maybe even "irrelevant."

But for two thousand years, the message of the cross has been the primary message of the church. We simply can't be true to our history or our calling if we downplay the death of Jesus and speak about other, more "relevant," topics. Christianity without a cross is just another religion, another system for trying to make it with God. Christianity *with* a cross is the best news ever sounded on planet Earth and reason to preach, teach, serve, and maybe even go to church committee meetings with joy.

In his second letter to the Corinthians, Paul spells out in further detail his motivation for ministry. He says he is compelled and challenged by the love of Christ, a love that proved itself at the cross. He says he has become a new creation, that old things have passed away and new things have arrived. Then he says this: "God was reconciling the world to himself through Christ, by not counting people's sins against them. He has trusted us with this message of reconciliation" (2 Cor 5:19). Throughout my ministry, I returned frequently to that verse to remember what I was supposed to be doing as a pastor.

Paul gives us at least four essentials for ministry in that one verse:

• *God has reconciled the world to himself.* The cross was about reconciliation, and, in the death of Jesus on the cross, the whole world was reconciled to God. Every last person, every last galaxy, every last created being was reconciled to God. They may not know it, believe it, or accept it, but Paul says it is true nonetheless. God has taken care of everyone and everything at the cross. We humans don't have to do anything but believe that and live in celebration of it.

• *This reconciliation came because of the death of Christ.* Other religions have truth and produce wonderful people. We Christians have much to learn from the other religions of the world and can never assume a haughty, know-it-all spirit. But we believe that Jesus was the unique revelation of God whose death made everything right. That's why Paul determined to know nothing but Jesus, and him crucified.

• *The death of Christ assures us once and for all of God's forgiveness.* Because of the cross, God no longer holds people's sins against them. In the Colossian letter, Paul writes, "He destroyed the record of the debt we owed, with its requirements that worked against us. He canceled it by nailing it to the cross" (Col 2:14). Those weren't just Jesus' hands being nailed to the cross that Friday afternoon; the law, with its burden and guilt, got nailed there, too.

• *God has committed to us the ministry of reconciliation.* This is our primary task—to tell this story, to declare the good news that God has fixed everything and everyone in Jesus Christ, to announce that we humans can live as free and forgiven creatures. We are called to say that reconciliation has happened and that it's time to embrace and celebrate it. We are one with God and with all of creation, so we can quit fighting and live at peace. Instead of putting on our worship bulletin the title "pastor," "youth minister," or "worship leader," we perhaps should all call ourselves "minister of reconciliation."

All of this is to remind us that Jesus' death sets our agenda and defines our message as ministers. We are not primarily growers of a religious institution, counselors who understand the intricacies of the human psyche, Bible scholars who have all of the answers to life's dilemmas, or jokesters who are the life of every party. Nor are we malleable puppets who let the world or the church tell us what is important.

No, we are men and women who remember the primacy of the cross. We are the ones who, in a culture that believes it to be outdated and irrelevant, dare to believe that the cross is the linchpin that holds everything together. We are the ones stubborn enough to preach and teach the cross, even when it is not popular.

Resurrection and the Power of Hope

The grand finale of Jesus' story is his resurrection from the dead. Had there been no resurrection, he would have been just another inspiring teacher who flashed on the screen of human history for a brief while and then was extinguished by powerful people. Without the resurrection, there would have been no church, no movement that came to be called Christianity, and no books like this one.

But the resurrection validated everything Jesus said about himself. It put a bold exclamation point at the end of his life. And it galvanized his early followers in dramatic fashion. Those same disciples who looked like bumbling, misguided, self-seeking followers became so bold and passionate that they were willing to die for the sake of Jesus. The very men who forsook him and fled when he died on the cross were willing to die on crosses themselves.

The difference? Jesus' resurrection from the grave. It not only validated everything Jesus said and did but was also the ultimate symbol of hope. If Jesus could conquer even death, what was there to fear?

Ever since the first Easter, those who know about it and celebrate it have been filled with hope. We find ourselves exulting with Paul, "Thanks be to God, who gives us this victory through our Lord Jesus Christ!" (1 Cor 15:57). Certainly we will all have to face crosses in our lives. Live long enough and your life will be lined with tombstones. People die. Dreams die. Relationships die. Life, ironically, is filled with death.

But those of us who get to minister in the name of a risen Lord have the privilege of being agents of hope amid all these deaths. We get to hold up before confused, grieving, unbelieving people the paradigm of the cross and resurrection. We get to declare that beyond every cross there is a resurrection. As we tiptoe with people through the tombstones, we're the ones who get to sing quietly in their ears, "If God is for us, who can be against us?" (Rom 8:31). In the midst of what looks like utter defeat, we get to whisper to them, "But in all these things we win a sweeping victory through the one who loved us" (Rom 8:37).

There were many times I said those things and wondered if they were really true. When I stood beside those parents whose fourteen-year-old son had taken his own life, it seemed like "pie in the sky by and by" to quote Scripture to them and tell them about a sweeping victory. There were times when I felt like the widow in one of John Masefield's poems who watched her son being executed and sobbed about "broken things, too broke to mend." Some things are so awful, so devastating they seem too broke to mend.

But even in that kind of terrifying darkness, there needs to be one person holding a candle of light. There needs to be someone who says kindly and confidently that God has taken on the ultimate enemy—death itself—and conquered it. There needs to be someone who says that if God is for us, nothing can defeat us. There needs to be one faithful soul who dares to say that, appearances to the contrary, nothing is too broke to mend.

The empty tomb has always been a source of hope for the believing community. Neuhaus, in *Freedom for Ministry*, underscores the necessity of holding it up for all to see—especially in times of grief:

> Recently I attended a funeral, and the pastor of the family involved had shared with them his knowledge about the stages of grief which he had culled from Kubler-Ross and others. Family members discussed with one another which stages they had passed through and where they now were on the spectrum. It was clinical. It was awful. Like patients in a doctor's office exchanging observations about their diseases. Much better an old-fashioned wake, with much food and drink and nostalgia and raging at the unfairness of it all, and reaffirming the fragile bonds between the living, and discovering again that through it all and in it all there is the quiet knowledge of a triumph that is somehow connected with a distant Easter morning in which all the threats to the present and the future were swallowed up in victory.[6]

Can you think of a higher calling than reminding people of the hope that still breaks out of that empty tomb? Can you think of a nobler task than being an agent of hope when the world is crashing down on someone? And that's precisely what we ministers get to do—at the hospital bedside, in the nursing home, at the jail cell, at the funeral home. We get to shine a little light into that dreadful darkness and try to lead people from the horror of the cross to the hope of the resurrection.

Agenda for Ministry

Unless we ministers have a clear understanding of who we are and what we are called to be and do, we will be tossed around by a multitude of whirlwinds—our own feelings of discouragement, the lure of the world's entanglements, and even, or maybe especially, the expectations of the church we serve.

In *No Place for Truth*, David Wells writes,

> The minister, like a small boat cast loose upon the high seas, has become vulnerable to a multitude of perils. Within the Church, strong winds are blowing from a range of religious consumers who look to the churches and ministers to meet their needs—and who quickly look elsewhere if they feel those needs are not being met. Basically, these consumers are looking for the sort of thing the self-movement is offering: they just want it in evangelical dress. A genuinely biblical and God-centered ministry is almost certain to collide head-on with the self-absorption and anthropocentric focus that are now normative in so many evangelical churches. The collisions take place in the soul of the minister and at the expense of his or her career.[7]

When those winds blow and those collisions come into our ministry, what gives us the courage and stability to stand firm? What keeps us from bolting for Tarshish? Or staying in Nineveh but accommodating to the needs of religious consumers? Where do we turn to remember who we really are and what we are really supposed to be doing?

I think we turn to the old, old story of Jesus. That familiar story gives us the identity we need if we are going to survive all the winds and collisions that are sure to come. When we get confused and discouraged about something at church, when an awful committee meeting looms on the horizon, when tending a lighthouse on a deserted island seems especially tempting to us . . .

• *What if we remembered Jesus' birth and the power of incarnational ministry?* What if we remembered that Jesus himself probably wanted to run from the bone-headed men he had chosen as his disciples?

• *What if we remembered Jesus' baptism and reaffirmed God's blessing on our lives and our ministry?* What if we rediscovered God's blessing on our own lives and renewed our calling to bless the people God places in our lives?

• *What if we remembered Jesus' teaching ministry and vowed to be poets using words to fashion a new world?* What if we recovered the value of both the Word and our own words?

• *What if we remembered Jesus' death and determined to know nothing among our people but Jesus Christ and him crucified?* What if we decided to live and proclaim the freedom and forgiveness that the cross brings into a person's life?

• *And what if we remembered Jesus' resurrection and determined to be agents of hope in an increasingly confusing and depressing society?* What if we dared to say that beyond every cross there is a resurrection?

If we could define ourselves that way, we might be able to stand even when the winds blow and the collisions come. We might be able to say to those who want us to try on the king's armor that it just doesn't fit us—that it will, in fact, probably lead to our death.

Armed only with the old, old story of Jesus and his love, we'll be able to pick up five smooth stones—unimpressive, ordinary-looking pebbles—and use them to slay whatever giants we have to face.

Notes

1. Eugene Peterson, *Working the Angles* (Grand Rapids MI: Eerdmans, 1987) 5.

2. Karl Olsson, *Come to the Party* (Waco: Word Books, 1972) 30–31.

3. M. Craig Barnes, *The Pastor as Minor Poet* (Grand Rapids MI: Eerdmans, 2009) 119.

4. Ibid., 13.

5. Ibid., 28.

6. Richard John Neuhaus, *Freedom for Ministry* (San Francisco: HarperSan-Francisco, 1979) 74.

7. David Wells, *No Place for Truth* (Grand Rapids MI: Eerdmans, 1993) 256.

Chapter 6

RIDING THE ROLLER COASTER: SURVIVING CHURCH CONFLICT

For centuries, Christians have been reading through Psalms as a devotional exercise, or even praying through the psalms as a way of enhancing their prayer lives. Should you ever decide to move sequentially through the psalms, I have one piece of advice to offer: Strap on a seatbelt before you begin.

Reading through the Psalms is a jarring experience. If we do it expecting to find one psalm after another praising God, we will be shocked at what we actually find. The psalmists—David in particular—take us on a roller coaster that is not for the faint of heart. There are psalms of praise, for sure, but there are also many psalms that are guaranteed to take us by surprise.

For example, we will read psalms of hate, calling down God's wrath on the psalmist's enemies. Psalms of confession and repentance, detailing tragic personal failures and seeking God's forgiveness. Psalms of confusion, wondering where in the world God went. Psalms of depression, expressing near despair. And psalms of petition, beseeching God to deliver the psalmist from his enemies.

It's that last category that I want to highlight here, those psalms where the psalmists acknowledge the pain of conflict and their need for God to help them deal with it. Here's a psalm of David that is typical of others in the Psaltery:

LORD, listen to my voice when I cry out—have mercy on me and answer me! Come, my heart says, seek God's face. LORD, I do seek your face! Please don't hide it from me! Don't push your servant aside angrily—you have been my help! God who saves me, don't neglect me! Don't leave me all alone! Even if my father and my mother left me all alone, the LORD would take me in. LORD, teach me your way; because of my opponents, lead me on a good path. Don't give me over to the desires of my enemies, because false witnesses and violent accusers have taken their stand against me. But I have sure faith that I will experience the LORD's goodness in the land of the living! Hope in the LORD! Be strong! Let your heart take courage! Hope in the LORD! (Ps 27:7-14)

We don't know what specific conflict precipitated that psalm of David, but it is clear he was feeling some major stress. He felt all alone. He felt under attack by his enemies. He felt surrounded by false witnesses and violent accusers. He was trying, in the midst of an awful, unnamed conflict, to trust God and to sense God's presence in his life.

I prayed that prayer many times when I was a pastor. Not those exact words, but those exact sentiments. When I looked out at the enemy surrounding my house some mornings, that's what I prayed. I felt all alone. I felt under attack. I felt surrounded by people who were doing harm to both my church and my serenity. I desperately needed to sense God's presence, to know I was not alone in my stress. It's bad enough being under a juniper tree, but even worse sensing that God is not there with you.

David's prayer in Psalm 27 provides us an opportunity to consider the thorny topic of church conflict. As I mentioned earlier in the book, I think conflict is the number one reason ministers leave churches and other places of Christian service. They get weary of dealing with angry, contentious people and decide to do something else. Their weariness is compounded by the belief that Christian people should be above pettiness, gossip, and mean-spiritedness. When they discover that Christians can be as difficult as any other group, these ministers conclude they might as well get abused in a secular system that at least pays a decent salary.

Before they submit their resignation, though, they earnestly try to handle their church's conflict in a positive way. They read books on conflict resolution, call meetings to try to get people to work out their differences, and embark on a personal plan for dealing with stress. In his book *Generation to Generation*, Edwin Friedman describes a plan he once saw for coping with stress and avoiding burnout:

- Find an outlet for working off stress.
- Talk to someone about your worries.
- Learn to accept what you cannot change.
- Try to balance the time between work and recreation.
- Be sure to get sufficient rest and sleep.
- Do one thing at a time instead of trying to tackle all of your tasks at once.
- Get out and make yourself available instead of sitting alone and feeling sorry for yourself.
- Do something for others.[1]

There's only one thing wrong with the suggestions on that list: they don't work! The beleaguered minister who moves through that list, trying to avoid burnout, will probably burn out. A list like that, as well intentioned as it is, only increases our guilt and frustration. We tried the recommended recipe for staving off burnout, and it didn't work. We think "Woe is me"—and off we go to find another line of work.

I would like to tell you that I found a foolproof plan for avoiding ministerial burnout, but I can't. I would also like to tell you that I learned to embrace conflict or, even better, to transform it into something positive. But that would be a lie. I did, however, learn to cope with conflict, and I did survive it—with only a handful of visible scars, a slight stutter, and a hand tremor that makes writing in long-hand almost impossible.

Though I never wrote down a strategy for surviving church conflict, I think I gradually pieced one together. I offer it to you not as a cure-all, but as a stimulus to get you to think about a strategy of your own.

Conflict Is Nothing New

There is at least a small measure of comfort in remembering that church conflict is nothing new. What you are experiencing at your church is what ministers have been experiencing for centuries. Churches throughout the ages have been famous for loving—and for fighting.

Those of us who preach on a regular basis have probably held up the early church as a model for our congregation. We have quoted Tertullian's famous line, "Behold, how they love one another!" to remind our people how much the early Christians loved each other and took care of each other. And that quote was no doubt accurate and true. The early Christians *did* love one another.

But just to be totally honest, we should also mention another quote—this one by the pagan historian Ammianus Marcellinus. Writing in the fourth century, he commented that the emperor Julian "quite rightly admonished the quarreling bishops of the Christians who had been introduced into the palace along with their divided people. He urged that each man should freely serve his own religion, forbidden by no one…. For he had learned that the hatred of wild beasts for man is less than the ferocity of most Christians toward one another."[2]

That's the way it was in the early church—the early Christians had love toward one another, and they had ferocity toward one another. Those of us who hold up the early church as a model of love and harmony need to read the New Testament again. Paul knew all about the ways in which Christians bite and devour one another (Gal 5), are overbearing and constantly fighting (1 Cor 1), are lacking in humility and understanding (1 Cor 8), and in various and sundry other ways show ferocity toward one another.

The chances are better than good that your church is the same way—full of both love and ferocity. That's the two-edged sword of church life. It is a community of compassion, and it is a community of contention. Those of us who minister in churches get to experience both edges of that sword.

On one hand, we get to be part of the community of compassion, shepherds in a flock of loving people. As church leaders, we often feel the wonder of the church, how much people love one another, and how much they serve and minister in their neighborhoods and towns. Beyond that, we often feel how much they love us and our families. We feel connected to something larger than ourselves, something full of genuine love. On those days, we thank God that we get to serve in such a community of compassion.

On the other hand, we have to be part of the community of contention, shepherds in a flock of quarreling people. From time to time, we are amazed that such a loving community of people can be so quickly transformed into petty, bickering, red-faced strangers. "Who are these people anyway?" we wonder in amazement. Is this the same woman who was serving soup in the soup kitchen last Saturday? Is this the same man who sat beside me at the football game a few weeks ago? How can such loving people become so ferocious? On those days, we ask God why we have to serve in such a community of contention.

Welcome to church life—in our age and every age. And that contention is especially hard to swallow because we know that Jesus told us that the world would know we belong to him because of the way we love one another.

Neuhaus writes,

> It must be admitted that there is no adequate preparation for the virulence of sheer nastiness that so often erupts in the life of the Christian community. It is a special sort of nastiness, perhaps because proximity to the sacred multiplies the force of the demonic. Envy, resentment, and unalloyed hatred can make their appearance in any human association, but they seem so ghastly in the Church because they so flagrantly contradict the stated purpose of the association.[3]

If you happen to be passing through a time of church conflict, take heart that you are but the latest in a long line of people who have had to glimpse the ghastly church conduct that so flagrantly contradicts its calling.

Your Church Conflict Is Nothing New

Knowing church history can help us put conflict into the proper context, but so can knowing our *own* church's history. I'm guessing that the conflict your church is currently experiencing is not its first siege of contention. I'm guessing that your church is like most churches—it has conflict embedded in its system.

In *Generation to Generation,* Friedman describes how cancer is transmitted in both the human body and in families and congregations:

> When it comes to the transmission of malignant processes, we may ask in what does cancer reside. The cells of the human body change rapidly from day to day and do almost a complete turnover every couple of years. It should not be surprising, therefore, that with families and congregations also, if there is a cancer in the system, the change-over in "cells" from year to year or from generation to generation will not necessarily affect a change in a malignant process. This is also why the transfusion of "new blood" or the performing of "major operations" rarely gets to the fundamental (systemic) problem.[4]

Again, knowing that your church has a history of conflict might not be particularly helpful (in fact, it might be terrifying!), but it does put your current crisis in perspective. The church has dissension in its blood, and it has little to do with you or your performance as a minister. If some other person were in your place, the dissension would still be present; the cancer would still be doing its dastardly work. The key is how to control the cancer, even conquer the cancer, so the system can become healthy again.

Friedman suggests that ministers can provide three key antidotes to return a system to health:

• First, *we can be healthy ourselves.* Friedman contends that "the overall health and functioning of any organization depend primarily on one or two people at the top."[5]

If the church is going to be healthy, we need to be healthy as leaders. Typically, a siege of church conflict sends everyone's health plummeting. Church leaders and church members all crumble in the face of dissension, and the whole system gets sicker and sicker. So it's crucial to try to stay healthy ourselves, to keep our perspective, to trust God, to keep preaching, serving, and loving. And to laugh as often as possible. If Friedman is right, the health of our church depends on how physically, emotionally, and spiritually healthy we are as individuals.

• Second, *we can be self-differentiated.* That means that we ministers stay true to who we are, voice our convictions, and lead in both word and example. It doesn't mean we become dogmatic or autocratic but that we define ourselves clearly and stay in touch with the congregation. If we can stay healthy and self-differentiated, Friedman says, the system will move toward health.

• Third, *we can be a non-anxious presence.* This might be the most difficult characteristic of all. Who can be a non-anxious presence with all of this chaos and contention in the air? It is not easy, for sure, but Friedman says,

> . . . the capacity of members of the clergy to contain their own anxiety regarding congregational matters, both those not related to them, as well as those where they became the identified focus, may be the most significant capability in their arsenal. Not only can such capacity enable religious leaders to be more clear-headed about solutions and more adroit in triangles but, because of the systemic effect that a leader's functioning always has on an entire organism, a nonanxious presence will modify anxiety throughout the entire congregation.[6]

If we can, with God's help, manage to stay healthy, self-differentiated, and a non-anxious presence, we might be able to fight off the cancer cells that are threatening to destroy both our church and our joy. And we might eventually be able to restore our church to robust health.

Don't Energize the Conflict

One way we ministers can foster those three qualities is to stay true to our calling, and our calling is not to be referees, mediators, or experts in conflict resolution. If we try to wear those hats, we are destined to be frustrated and, paradoxically, we will feed the very conflict we're trying to heal. When we decide to "take the bull by the horns" and address the conflict head-on, we end up unintentionally energizing the forces of dissension in the system.

If you have conflict raging in your church or organization, I can give you some tried-and-true ways to make that conflict even worse:

- Confront one of the people who is fomenting the dissension and have a "knock-down-drag-out" about the issue in question.
- Have a "team-building" session with your staff or the particular group that is at odds.
- Use proven "team-building techniques" for fostering group harmony.
- Call a series of meetings to discuss the conflict and to "group think" about how to end it.
- Preach a series of sermons on *koinonia* and how to develop it in a church.
- Lead a series of Bible studies or Sunday school lessons on church conflict and how to end it.
- Spend an inordinate amount of time in committee meetings, church council meetings, deacons' meetings, and other official church gatherings discussing what is wrong with the church and what needs to be done to fix it.

In other words, if you want to make the conflict even worse than it is, talk about it constantly. Shine the spotlight of attention on it every chance you get. Ironically, the more you focus on the problem, the more energy you give it. The church becomes totally self-absorbed, and the true purpose of the church gets lost in a barrage of well-intentioned "team-building" activities.

Shall we, then, play ostrich-in-the-sand and pretend the conflict doesn't exist? Shall we place our hands over our ears and say to the screaming cries of dissension, "I can't hear you?" Well, no. We have to answer honest questions, seek to be peacemakers, and keep reminding the church of its true calling.

But we don't have to drown in the conflict. If we get mired in it as leaders, that's exactly what will happen—we will drown. We will be totally out of our element because we're not trained mediators (and don't want to be!), and we will unwittingly pour gasoline on the fire of anger that is already burning in the church. We will sink into despair and likely take the church with us.

No, in the midst of conflict, we can remember who we are and what we are called to do. And we can stay true to that calling. If we can remain healthy, self-differentiated, and a non-anxious presence, then those who are with us are more than those who are with them.

Don't Over-Promise

Closely aligned with the notion of not focusing on conflict lest we energize it is the equally true notion that we shouldn't focus too much on the church as a "family." Sounding the note of church oneness too often reveals two things about us.

First, it reveals that we probably don't have church harmony. I once had a friend who put a bumper sticker on his car that read, "I love my wife." When I saw that bumper sticker, I feared for my friend's marriage. If you truly love your wife, you don't put it on a bumper sticker. Bumper-sticker love is a classic case of "protesting too much." Sure enough, he and his wife were divorced in a few years.

In a similar way, the more we talk about community, harmony, oneness, and *agape* in our churches, the more we reveal we don't have those things. We're protesting too much, preaching too much, teaching too much about the love Christians are supposed to have for one another. If we have that love, we really don't have to put it on a bumper sticker.

Second, it reveals that we're guilty of promising more than we might be able to deliver. When we repeatedly say that the church is a "family" and that we're all "one in the Spirit," we could be fostering disillusionment in the church. I'm convinced that people occasionally leave churches because they feel like the church simply isn't a family to them when they need a family.

Every Sunday the church has been advertising itself as a family, a community, a place to belong, and so forth, but these people don't feel the closeness that is being advertised, so they move on. Of course, their new church won't be their family, either, so they will likely just keep moving from church to church until they finally give up and quit the church altogether.

Community doesn't happen because we sing about it every Sunday or because the preacher says we're supposed to have it. Community happens when two people mysteriously connect with each other. When that happens, something sacred and wonderful has taken place. But we can't command it, and we can't promise it to all who enter our church.

When we do try to command it and promise it, we're sowing seeds of disenchantment and conflict. Some people inevitably will be disappointed and decide to try to find a "church family" elsewhere.

Remember the Leverage of the Dependent

Family systems theorists have a concept they call "the leverage of the dependent." By that they mean that the most dependent, troubled people in any system tend to wield the most power. In families, churches, offices, classrooms, and other organizations, the most dependent, least qualified people are calling the shots.

That means the other people in that system are doing a careful dance to placate the dependent person among them. The family dances around the one child who is angry and unruly. The classroom accommodates to the desires of the most demanding student in the class. The office tiptoes around the angriest employee lest there be a scene. And the church, in an attempt to foster harmony, bends over backwards to please a few disgruntled people.

Most of us who live in families, classrooms, offices, and churches know all about the leverage of the dependent. We have seen it with our own eyes and experienced it firsthand. The sad result is that these systems can't function as smoothly as they should or accomplish as much as they could. Because the most dependent people in these systems have the leverage, the systems are destined to be less than they could be.

This is a frustrating phenomenon to the others in the system, but it is even more frustrating to those who lead it. The parents in that family, the teacher in that classroom, the boss in that office, and the ministers in that church will be pulling their hair out because those groups keep underachieving.

The leader who knows about the leverage of the dependent can do two things to make the system more efficient. First, the leader can begin to focus on the other members of the group and not give all the attention to the dependent ones. For church leaders, that means we don't focus all our time and effort on a few demanding people in the church. We start focusing on the healthy ones, the ones who can keep the church moving forward in service and ministry. We stop dancing around a few surly people and encourage the healthy ones to flourish.

Second, the leader can be self-differentiated and keep defining herself and her vision for the church. We are in a community of faith, and everyone in that community has a voice, but the leader is charged with the responsibility of articulating the purpose and vision of the church lest detractors pull it off course.

Friedman writes,

An organism tends to function best when its "head" is well-differentiated. The key to successful spiritual leadership, therefore, with success understood not only as moving people toward a goal, but also in terms of the survival of the family (and its leader), has more to do with the leader's capacity for self-definition than with the ability to motivate others.[7]

Just knowing about the leverage of the dependent can help us deal with its destructive effects. We can't remove all the dependent people from our church, but we can reduce some of their power. By focusing on the healthy folks among us and clearly defining ourselves and our church's purpose, we can at least stay on course. And those who will appreciate our ministry the most will be the healthy ones who have been frustrated for years at the church's underperformance.

People Leaving the Church Is Not Always Bad

Since some of these dependent people are likely to pack up and leave, this seems to be an appropriate time to mention that people leaving the church is not always a bad thing. It might be a move that benefits both the person who leaves and the church that gets left.

Of course, we never want that to happen. We want everyone to be happy, feel community among us, and spend their whole lives being a part of our church. But we also know that this will not happen for everyone. Some people will grow disenchanted, maybe even angry, and when they do, bad things will start to happen—both in that individual and in the church as a whole. Miserable people make people miserable, and these disenchanted, angry folks will start sowing seeds of misery in the church.

I spent the last thirty-three years of my ministry pastoring two churches. In both of those churches, we had situations where people grew disenchanted. One woman came to my office to tell me how miserable she was in our church. She said she got knots in her stomach in every worship service. I simply acknowledged to her what she already knew—church is not supposed to put knots in your stomach. It's not supposed to make you miserable. Shortly thereafter, she and her family left our church and joined another church in our city. Several other families quickly and quietly did the same.

But, as far as I can tell, their leaving was a good thing—for them and for our church. Most of these people found other churches—presumably churches that didn't put knots in their stomachs—and found avenues for worship and ministry. And our church immediately got "happier" without these miserable people among us. Those who left us did well, and the church did well. I think it was a classic "win-win" situation.

There are times in the midst of church conflict when we pray that God will change certain people's hearts so that they can stay among us and be in harmony. If the conflict continues to fester, we might get to the point that we pray that God will impress upon these people that they need to worship and minister somewhere else. If and when that prayer gets answered, it can be a blessing to all concerned.

Not All Conflict Is Bad

As much as I disliked conflict and tried to avoid it at all costs, I eventually came to see that not all conflict was negative and destructive. There were times when conflict served to draw people together. On the far side of their differences, they found a new understanding and appreciation for one another.

If we want to assure that we never have church conflict, we could simply agree that all members will (1) never bring up any controversial issue, (2) never say anything that might be controversial or "outside the box," and (3) never disagree with a church leader or staff member. If every member will agree to do those three simple things, church conflict will disappear.

But real community will disappear, too. Can we hope to have true oneness as a church if we always avoid controversy, are afraid to say what we really believe, or feel intimidated by our church's leaders? We might not have conflict if we had those rules, but we wouldn't have a church either; we would have a cult. The only way to have a church is for members to be who they are, say what they believe, and challenge authority if they feel the need.

So, like it or not, we can't have community without the possibility of conflict. If we grant people the freedom to be themselves and declare themselves, we have to live with the possibility—no, the inevitability—of conflict.

But on the far side of conflict, there is often deeper community. Once people have been given the freedom to speak their minds and voice their opinions, there is at least the possibility of intimacy. They have gone out on a limb and revealed who they are and what they believe, and the church has embraced them and taken them seriously. On the far side of the conflict, we might have to agree to disagree, but we may feel closer to one another than we ever have before.

For thirty-eight years as a pastor, I always dreaded conflict. But I occasionally did get to see the blessings that came from it.

Don't Let Conflict Lead to Contempt

Conflict takes a heavy toll on any church or religious organization. It can sap the life and enthusiasm out of any member caught in the middle of it. It can especially sap the life and enthusiasm out of the ministers who lead those churches and organizations. If dissension lingers too long, it can prompt those leaders to start feeling anger and contempt for the very people they are supposed to love and serve. The hostility swirling around in the system has to go somewhere, and leaders can easily start directing it at the congregation itself.

Neuhaus writes,

> . . . it is precisely our passion for change that must stir up the gift of love. We all know how insidiously it happens that a pastor begins—perhaps at first unconsciously—to assume an adversary posture toward his people, to speak of "them" as the enemy. Then it is forgotten that prophecy is an office of love and not of contempt. Then it is forgotten that Amos, Hosea, and others spoke so straightforwardly precisely because they loved so recklessly, thinking so much more of the people of God than they thought of themselves. Then it is forgotten that the prophetic and priestly ministries are not antithetical but are forged together by the knowledge that whom we would change we must first love.[8]

When we sense that conflict is producing contempt in us, it is time to repent. It is time to remind ourselves that we can't lead people or change people if we don't first love them. If we find it impossible to love them, if the conflict has so tarnished our spirits that we are bitter and mad at the "enemy," it is time to consider leaving the church ourselves. No minister who is full of contempt for a church, or even a small fraction of a church, can lead that church to wholeness.

Bluebirds on the Windowsill

I began this chapter with the suggestion that all who plan to read through Psalms would be wise to strap on a seatbelt because they're going to be riding an emotional roller coaster. I think the same thing holds true for anyone contemplating a life of ministry in the church or some other Christian organization. A life of ministry is going to be a rough roller coaster ride, and we need to be aware of that before we ever begin.

Anyone who ministers in the name of Christ gets to experience some ecstatic "highs"—stirring worship experiences, life-changing ministry opportunities, being connected to a community of love, using your best gifts and talents for the glory of God, standing with people at the crucial junctures of their lives, feasting at church suppers, proclaiming the truth to people who will actually listen, and a host of others. There were many days as a pastor when my breath was taken away by the awesome privilege of getting to be a minister of the gospel. Thank God for those ministerial mountaintops!

But anyone who ministers in the name of Christ also has to experience some miserable "lows"—useless committee meetings about trivial issues, worship services that fall flat, choirs that sing flat, immature people who wreak havoc on everyone around them, long business meetings about insignificant things, and arguments and conflicts about everything from the color of the carpet in the sanctuary to the proposed salary for the youth minister. As I have already mentioned, there were days as a pastor when I yearned to be running a bookstore or bed and breakfast. The view from under the juniper tree can make any non-ministerial job look alluring.

In her book, *Leaving Church*, Barbara Brown Taylor writes honestly about her departure from her church in Georgia. Conflict played a big part in her decision to leave that church, and she describes the discouragement and disillusionment she experienced because of the conflict. Finally, as her book's title indicates, she decided to leave the church and move in a different vocational direction.

Here's the way she describes where she was emotionally and spiritually when she opted to leave:

> Above all, I saw that my desire to draw as near to God as I could had backfired on me somehow. Drawn to care for hurt things, I had ended up with compassion fatigue. Drawn to a life of servanthood, I had ended up a service provider. Drawn to marry the Divine Presence, I had ended up estranged. Like the bluebirds that sat on my windowsills at home, pecking at the reflections they saw in the glass, I could not reach the greenness for which my soul longed. For years I had believed that if I had just kept at it, the

glass would finally disappear. Now, for the first time, I wondered if I had devoted myself to an illusion.[9]

The words and phrases she uses in that paragraph describe all too well the toll that conflict exacts upon many who minister in the church: "backfired," "compassion fatigue," "service provider," "estranged," "illusion." But her book title probably says it most clearly. Conflict has convinced many men and women that they need to try "leaving church" so they can find joy somewhere else.

We will turn our attention in the next chapter to that difficult issue. How do we know when it's time to leave? What are the signals that warn us we need to leave the church and use our gifts and talents elsewhere? What do we do when we find ourselves out of gas on a lonely road and not sure where to turn next?

Notes

1. Edwin Friedman, *Generation to Generation* (New York: The Guilford Press, 1985) 216–17.

2. Quoted in K. Morrison, *Tradition and Authority in Western Christianity* (Princeton: Princeton University Press, 1969) 106.

3. Richard John Neuhaus, *Freedom for Ministry* (San Francisco: HarperSanFrancisco, 1979) 106.

4. Friedman, *Generation to Generation*, 198.

5. Ibid., 221.

6. Ibid., 208.

7. Neuhaus, *Freedom for Ministry*, 14.

9. Barbara Brown Taylor, *Leaving Church* (San Francisco: HarperSanFrancisco, 2006) 102.

Chapter 7

LIVING IN TEL-ABIB: LEAVING THE STEEPLE

The prophet Ezekiel's ministry didn't unfold at all the way he thought it would. He thought he was going to be a priest in Jerusalem, doing priestly things in the temple. His name meant "God strengthens," and that is what he thought he would spend his life doing—being a source of strength to people who came to the temple needing a godly priest.

But his life careened in a radically different direction in 598 BC, while he was still in his twenties. King Nebuchadnezzar of Babylon sent an army to Jerusalem to quell a rebellion, and the results were disastrous to Judah. The king of Judah, Jehoiakim, was killed, and his son, Jehoiachin, surrendered to the Babylonians to spare the city. Jehoiachin and other leaders were deported to Babylon, and among those deported was the young priest Ezekiel. As far as we know, he never returned to Jerusalem.

Eleven years later, the Babylonians destroyed the temple and much of Jerusalem, and many citizens of Judah were carried off to Babylon. When they got there, Ezekiel was there to greet them and to strengthen them in their time of need. Certainly, he never envisioned this kind of ministry. He thought he would be in Jerusalem, not Babylon. And he thought he would have a ministry in the temple, not along the grassy shores of the Chebar River. But that is where he ended up, and that is where he ministered. Ezekiel was destined to serve God not under the steeple but among wounded people on the fringes of life.

At one point he tried to describe what was going on in his life and ministry:

> Then the wind lifted me up, and I heard behind me a great quaking sound from his place. Blessed is the LORD's glory! The sound was the creatures' wings beating against each other and the sound of the wheels beside them; it was a great rumbling noise. Then the wind picked me up and took me away. With the LORD's power pressing down against me I went away, bitter and deeply angry, and I came to the exiles who lived beside the Chebar River at Tel-abib. I stayed there among them for seven desolate days. (Ezek 3:12-15)

What jumps out to me in this text is its ambiguity. Ezekiel was keenly aware of the Lord's presence and glory there by the Chebar River. But he was also bitter and deeply angry. And, frankly, who can blame him? This is not what he signed on for, and he would have preferred to be in Jerusalem enjoying the life of a temple priest. But, in spite of his bitterness, he was determined to be faithful to God and to his fugitive parishioners there in Tel-abib.

Ezekiel's experience has proven not to be unique. I know many people who envisioned for themselves a life under the steeple—preaching sermons, leading worship, serving Communion, and attending to all the institutional duties a church minister has to perform. But that is not the way life unfolded for them. As with Ezekiel, unexpected factors crashed into their lives and sent them on a completely different path. They assumed they would spend their lives in the temple in Jerusalem but found themselves instead on the Chebar River doing unforeseen things with unforeseen people.

With Ezekiel's story in our minds, let's consider in this chapter the troubling, mostly avoided topic of when to leave Jerusalem and head to Babylon. How do we know when it's time to leave the church? How can we discern when God is leading us to move in a new direction in our ministry? And, if we do leave, what can we expect to happen next?

Leaving the Steeple

Some ministers leave the church for the same reason Ezekiel left the temple—an unforeseen catastrophe shattered their church career and sent them to their own version of Babylon. Perhaps they were waylaid by health problems that made church life too demanding. Perhaps they stumbled into a depression that rendered them unable to help anyone else. Perhaps they suffered a divorce that destroyed both their family and their standing in the church. Perhaps some moral failure on their part ruined their reputation and effectiveness in the church. The list of possible catastrophes that can befall ministers is almost endless. These ministers leave Jerusalem for Babylon not because they *want* to but because they *have* to.

But I'm thinking now of ministers who are so beat up and run down by their current place of service that they're thinking seriously of trying some other line of work. They're feeling so discouraged and disillusioned, they're thinking of leaving the church. They feel called to minister, they were confident that God would be with them in all they undertook, and they have done their best in the ministerial field they were called to tend. But it hasn't worked. The church is failing, and, maybe even worse, their own spiritual lives are failing. The spiral, both institutionally and personally, is definitely downward.

These ministers can easily identify with Barbara Brown Taylor:

Having tried as hard as I knew how to seek and serve Christ in all persons, I knew for sure that I could not do it. I was not even sure that I wanted to do it anymore, and I felt increasingly deceitful saying that I would. Feeding people was no longer feeding me. While I remained constitutionally incapable of walking past a hungry baby bird, it was the wild geese that were calling to me. When I heard them coming, I hurried to the window, straining to see them through the branches of the tall pines overhead. Sometimes all I caught was a beating wing or an outstretched neck, but even that was enough to set me weeping again. No thoughts went with the tears. The tears simply fell out of my eyes, and it was not until the geese were gone that the words formed in the empty air. *Take me with you.*[1]

When the tears fill our eyes and the geese beckon us to take up wings and escape our current place of ministry, it is time (past time?) to give careful thought to our future. It would be nice if there were simple tests we could take that would tell us when it is time to leave the steeple and do something else, but I don't know of any. Come to think of it, if I did know of any, I wouldn't trust them anyway.

But there are some hints and clues that can at least help us make an informed decision. As we try to get an accurate picture of our soul and our place of ministry, we can evaluate where we are on several personal scales or continuums. Consider seven of these and try to place yourself somewhere on each one.

Love and Resentment. This is the tension I mentioned earlier. On one hand, we know we are to love the church and that we can't lead the church if we don't love it. On the other hand, we can get to a point where that love is impossible. We have such estrangement from certain people that we just can't love them.

At some nebulous point on this continuum, the resentment starts to eat at our souls as well as our relationships, and we grow increasingly bitter and negative. The situation degenerates into "us" and "them," with little or no chance of reconciliation. We are conflicted over our inability to love these people, and the church itself becomes conflicted. Before all of that conflict takes its inevitable toll, it is better for all concerned if we leave and find another place to serve.

Dreams and Memories. Before I retired, I had lunch with a friend and told him I was considering retirement but wasn't sure it was the right time. He told me something that was helpful to me and applies, I think, to any minister who is considering leaving a church. He said someone once told him that it's time to leave a church when your memories outnumber your dreams.

As I thought about my long ministry at that church, I concluded that was precisely my situation. I was filled with good memories, but my dreams were in short supply. When it came to dreaming dreams and seeing visions, I was spent. I decided that both for my sake and the sake of the church I served, it was time to retire and shift my focus. I needed a new dream, and the church needed a pastor with dreams and visions for its future.

Somewhere along this continuum, our memories start outweighing our dreams, and we start to sense that it is time to go. Where there is no vision, the people (and the minister) perish.

Contentment and Calling. There may be no greater tension in ministry than the tension between our contentment and our calling. We feel that we are called by God to serve others, and we know that this call comes with certain risks. We know, in fact, that anyone whose Lord died on a cross can hardly expect following him to be a bed of roses. So we determine to be faithful even when the going gets tough.

But we also know that if we don't have joy in our hearts as we serve, our ministry will be of little value to anyone. Our joy is what validates and empowers our ministry. Craig Barnes writes, "The pastor is left with only having to attend to the quiet joy that lies beneath the pathos of his or her own story with Christ. If it isn't true for the pastor, why should anyone else believe the Gospel the pastor proclaims?"[2] We know that is true. If there is no quiet joy in our own story with Christ, what we say will ring empty and false.

What do we do when that joy is gone, when, as Barbara Brown Taylor so aptly puts it, "our role and our soul are eating each other alive"?[3] At some point, we may have to sacrifice the role to save the soul.

Growth and Stagnation. My joking comment earlier—about passing through small Texas towns and remarking that a person could "die on the vine" there—is not really all that funny. The truth is, pastors and church leaders *do* die on the vine there. They also die on the vine in suburban and city churches.

One reason for this stagnation is that church leaders think they have to "dumb down" the truth so that increasingly theologically illiterate people can comprehend it. Pastors would like to soar with the theological eagles in their sermons, but on close scrutiny, realize there are no such eagles sitting in the pews. So they scale it back, say what they have said for thirty years, and try to communicate with people on a primary level.

Eventually, these pastors get tired of saying the same things over and over again. They long to go deeper in the things of the Spirit and yearn for a few kindred souls who will go with them. If they never get to leave theological kindergarten, though, they will start to wither and die—and possibly decide to do something else. And in nearly every church there are many people who would love to leave kinder-garten, too, if only their preacher would lead the way.

Gifts and Guilt. When I first got to college, I decided to major in accounting. I was reasonably good with numbers, and I had an uncle who was an accountant and seemed to enjoy what he was doing, so I thought accounting might fit me, too.

I took an accounting class my first semester and found it both boring and difficult. I took another accounting class my second semester and confirmed in my own mind that I was not cut out to be an accountant after all. It might have been right for my uncle, but it wasn't right for me. So I changed majors and became much happier.

Something like that happens to ministers, too. They're reason-ably spiritual people and well spoken, and they know pastors and church leaders who have flourished under the steeple, so they decide that is what they want to do. But then ten days, or ten months, or ten years into their ministry, they conclude that they were wrong. Their particular gifts don't match up with what they have to do every day.

Once they come to that realization, they can either stay in the church out of guilt (Who, after all, can bear the shame of disap-pointing both God and Mom and Dad?), or they can face up to the truth and find a place that *does* match their particular gifts and abilities.

Ironically, leaving the church is for some ministers a positive response to God's call and a giant step toward finding God's will.

Conviction and Doubt. The poet John Keats once described the importance of "negative capability" for the writing of poetry: "Nega-tive capability is when man is capable of being in uncertainties, mysteries, and doubt without any irritable reaching after fact and reason."[4]

Almost daily, Christian ministers have to walk among wreckage and deal with things that make no sense at all. Why does God allow children to die? Why this hurricane or this tornado? Why doesn't God say or do something when life tumbles in? There is no "fact and reason" for such things, so the minister who has a chance of surviving this chaos is the one who has cultivated negative capability. He or she can deal with uncertainties, mysteries, and doubt and not become irritable or try to explain them in three-point sermons or PowerPoint presentations.

But negative capability happens only when ministers have deeply held convictions relating to the sovereignty of God. We can walk among the wreckage and deal with the mysteries as long as we trust in the sovereignty of a loving God. If we lose that trust, we have little to offer anyone else. As Barnes puts it, "When the sheep of our flock are in the midst of their frightening losses, they need to lean upon our faith and our trust that they are not abandoned to this destruction. They need to believe that at least we believe."[5]

Honesty and Orthodoxy. In his book *Not Sure,* pastor John Suk candidly struggles with the tension between honesty and orthodoxy. Increasingly, he felt a wide gulf growing between what he believed and what he knew he was *supposed* to believe:

> I had the public face of a true-blue evangelical pastor as always, but in my private life I was asking more and more questions and beginning to suspect that the answers I was entertaining were not all acceptable to the powers that be. The simple oneness of my childhood was forever fractured. I was no longer sure, and I knew it.[6]

Once again, this is a "role and soul" struggle. Our role demands that we believe one thing, but our soul demands that we believe something else. If the dissonance between role and soul gets too severe, it is time to look long and hard at what we're doing. Nothing—not even our role as a minister in the church—is more important than tending our soul and being faithful to the difference to which we have been called.

In the best of all worlds, we spend our entire ministries on the left side of those seven tensions. We love what we're doing and the people we're doing it with. We have dreams for our ministries that energize us and the church or organization we serve. We find great joy in ministry and can't imagine doing anything else. We're growing spiritually and emotionally and developing personal substance and depth. We're getting to use our gifts and abilities and feel we're doing a good job in our ministry. We have strong convictions about the sovereignty of God that enable us to walk among the uncertainties, mysteries, and doubt that we encounter every day. And we can honestly be who we are and declare what we believe with no hesitation.

Now, would all who find yourselves on the left side of all of those tensions please raise your hand? If I have just described your current ministry, would you now identify yourself? Just as I thought—I see no hands raised. If you do have your hand in the air, count your many blessings and express your gratitude to God every day. I think most who minister in the church or in some other Christian group find themselves dealing with some ambiguity in several of those areas.

And there is some indefinable moment, known only by the suffering minister, when a tipping point is reached. When the resentment gets too heavy, when the dreams are too few and far between, when the misery becomes too acute, when the stagnation gets unbearable, when the guilt can no longer hide the absence of gifts, when the doubts overwhelm the convictions, or when the need to be honest trumps the need to be orthodox, it might be time to leave the steeple and find a parish elsewhere.

It might be God's way of getting you out of Jerusalem so you can make a difference in Tel-abib. It might even be God's way of saving your sanity. In the memorable words of Walter Brueggemann, "The world for which you have been so carefully prepared is being taken away from you . . . by the grace of God."[7]

Who Are You Going to Be Tomorrow?

Some ministers will struggle with those issues and decide they should leave their current church or place of ministry and move to another church or place of ministry. They'll stay under the steeple and try to make it work elsewhere. Others will do what I did five years ago—retire and look for new ways to be both joyful and useful.

But some will opt to leave the steeple altogether. They will decide they are too hurt and scarred to continue. And they're afraid that moving to another steeple will only continue the abuse there. So they will opt out and then have to decide what to do next.

Some words from the novelist Reynolds Price will likely resonate with them. After surviving both cancer and the treatments that went with it, he said this in an interview in the *Oxford Review*:

> When you undergo huge traumas in middle life, everybody is in league with us to deny that the old life has ended. Everybody is trying to patch us up and get us back to who we were, when in fact what we need to be told is, You're dead. Who are you going to be tomorrow?[8]

That's the way you feel when you leave the church—dead. But the intriguing question that comes next is, Who are you going to be tomorrow? What if God has closed one door so that another one can be opened? What if you needed this death so you could find a resurrected life on the other side of it? What if your ministry is not over but just beginning?

As mentioned, I spent periodic times under the juniper tree when I was a pastor and occasionally dreamed of doing something else. But I never seriously thought about leaving the church, so I can't write authoritatively about life after the church—except as a happily retired pastor who spends his afternoons sipping coffee and dispensing wisdom from a laptop at Starbucks. I've never experienced the pain and death of walking away from the steeple, so take what I have to say with a grain of salt. My scars are nothing compared to the scars some of my minister friends have.

Two simple thoughts come to mind when I think of how best to survive life without church. The first one is *keep your eyes open*. We're all magnets that naturally attract certain people and experiences just by being who we are. Instead of frantically seeking a new place of ministry or new people to relate to, why not just open your eyes and pay attention to who and what comes your way? Why not just be the magnet you already are and see what happens?

When I was pondering retirement, I wondered what I would do next. I thought I knew some of the pieces of the puzzle, for sure: stay in our house in San Antonio, return as a "regular member" to our church once the dust had settled, teach religion part-time at a local college, and continue to write. But beyond that, I wasn't sure what retirement would look like for me. When I announced my resignation to the church, I said I planned to "teach and write."

Then, life happened and that blueprint went out the window. We decided to move to the Austin area to be closer to our children and grandchildren, which meant, of course, that we couldn't stay in our house in San Antonio or return to our former church. I quickly lost all interest in being an adjunct professor and dropped the idea of teaching religion. I did continue to write—which I love doing—and even added more writing assignments to my schedule.

So here I am, five years into retirement, surprised at where I am and what I'm doing. I just let things happen and kept my eyes open, and I would like to believe that what has happened to us has been more than accidental. We have a new home, new opportunities to be with our kids and grandkids, a new church, new neighbors—indeed, a whole new life. And I get to sit here at Starbucks and suggest that you try the same approach. In your death, keep your eyes open and see who and what comes your way. And see if resurrection comes, too.

To put it succinctly, you might not have to choose your next ministry; it might choose you.

The second thing I would say is *keep your heart open.* That could be a much tougher assignment. Anyone who feels beat up by the church has some "heart issues" to deal with. How do you keep your heart open when it's been battered shut by a host of "good Christians"? How do you keep your heart open when even God, the source of love and grace, has left you sitting in darkness? Who wouldn't close their heart in such a desolate situation? Who wouldn't join Elijah under that solitary juniper tree?

The only way to survive that misery is to start prying our heart open by reclaiming some truths we have said we believe and now get to find out if we really do:

• *Grace reigns supreme, even here under the juniper tree.* Our worth doesn't depend on our performance. We love God *because* God first loved us. Before we ever preached a sermon, taught a class, visited a sick person, or went on a mission trip, we were loved as much as God could love us. Now that we're feeling beat up and cast out, we're held in that grace—even if we don't feel it. Grace is not just a theological concept; it is a reality that we get to experience in times like these.

• *Ministry happens in the most unlikely places and to the most unlikely people.* We have so institutionalized Christianity in our day that we've made ministry far more formal and structured than it truly is. Ministry doesn't have to be in the annual budget and have church approval. Ministry is taking a pot of soup to your neighbor. Playing catch with the kid next door. Writing a compelling sentence. Listening to your spouse with undivided attention. It's not big, formal, and churchy; it's small, informal, and personal. We get to redefine ministry now that we no longer have to "go through church channels."

• *The will of God involves more than what we do for a living.* I have long loved Robert Capon's definition of the will of God: "The will of God is not a list of stops for us to make to pick up mouthwash, razor blades and a pound of chopped chuck on the way home. It is his longing that we will take the risk of being nothing but ourselves, desperately in love."[9] As long as we believe that the will of God has to do only with our job in an institutional expression of Christianity, we will be stuck under the juniper tree. We will have to conclude that we've missed the will of God for our lives, that we have failed miserably in living up to that will. But if the will of God is about taking the risk of being nothing but ourselves, desperately in love, then what we are doing now might be squarely in the middle of God's love. Our challenge is to keep being ourselves and to stay in love with life, God, and a few people.

• *God has never been confined to the temple.* Ironically, those of us who have preached this the loudest are the ones who deny it most when we are no longer working in the temple. We have said repeatedly that God is out there in the world, not here in the church, and we have implored church people to get out there in the world to make a difference. But once we're no longer under the steeple, we act as if our ministry is over. Really? Whatever happened to God being out there in the world? Shouldn't we now see our role as ministers to a world where God lives and moves and has his being?

The answer to the question as to who we will be tomorrow is not one we can spell out clearly. Stripped of our churchly garments, we feel naked and exposed, and we have no idea where, or even *if,* we will land on our feet. Without church support (financially and emotionally), we might collapse like a flimsy house of cards.

But if we can keep our eyes open and let things happen, and if we can keep our heart open and really believe those truths that we have always claimed to believe, we can survive. We can not only survive but even thrive. We can discover that God is more real outside the church than inside.

What Is Saving Your Life?

I have a friend who bears many more church scars than I have. As a pastor in the tumultuous sixties, he left his church during a conflict over racial issues. He took a stand for integration, which so angered some church members that he had to leave.

He went to another church and began having problems in his marriage. Eventually, he and his wife decided to divorce, which necessitated his departure from that church. Divorced pastors in those days were anathema.

My friend eventually remarried and became a personal counselor for several years before becoming pastor of another church. This time the issue of homosexuality reared its divisive head and split the church, which sent my friend and his wife packing. To heal, they hit the road and lived out of a travel trailer for months. The doctor told him if he had stayed in that last church, he would have developed serious health problems.

Not many pastors have had to deal with racism, divorce, and homosexuality in successive churches like my friend. But nearly every pastor or minister of any kind has horror stories to share if you only take the time to listen. Ministerial scars are everywhere if you know how to spot them.

But what I want to tell you about my friend is that he never despaired. He somehow survived all of those crises, shifted his focus to teaching, and became a college professor. Now in his eighties, he is still teaching college classes, still believing in God, and still full of life and laughter. The scars haven't destroyed him; they've empowered him. Every day he heads to class to teach college students. He is being saved by doing exactly what he wants to be doing and what he feels he is called to do. He is living proof to me that there is life—life abundant—after the steeple.

In *Leaving Church*, Barbara Brown Taylor testifies to the same reality. After leaving her church, she became a professor at Piedmont College and says about this transition:

> Teaching school is saving my life now. While I am still in charge of my classroom, I am not God's designated representative in my students' lives. They can take me or leave me, and few need me to authorize their understanding of how the world works. Because we do not rely on one another for ultimate meaning, we are able to talk about things that might be too hot for us to handle if we were more dependent on one another. Our covenant exists on a syllabus, not a Bible, which allows us to ask unorthodox questions of one another. Since we are in a classroom and not a church, we are free to wonder instead of witness. Our answers change from day to day, as we too are changed by listening to one another. Compared to church, this may not be real community, but real transformation still happens in it.[10]

That is the hope of every minister who decides to walk away from the church or from some other institutional expression of Christianity. The hope is that, like my friend and like Barbara Brown Taylor, something or someone will save us. We will find something—or, better said, be found by something—that will fill us with meaning and joy. On the far side of our disappointment and disillusionment, there will be enchantment and enthusiasm.

Like Ezekiel, we will find that in leaving the temple we will discover precisely where we were supposed to be all the time.

Notes

1. Barbara Brown Taylor, *Leaving Church* (San Francisco: HarperSanFrancisco, 2006) 113.

2. M. Craig Barnes, *The Pastor as Minor Poet* (Grand Rapids MI: Eerdmans, 2009) 48.

3. Taylor, *Leaving Church*, 111.

4. *John Keats: Selected Letters*, ed. Robert Gittings (New York: Oxford University Press, 2002) 41.

5. Barnes, *The Pastor as Minor Poet*, 48.

6. John Suk, *Not Sure* (Grand Rapids MI: Eerdmans, 2011) 66.

7. Quoted in Taylor, *Leaving Church*, 122.

8. Ibid., 221.

9. Robert Farrar Capon, *Hunting the Divine Fox* (New York: Seabury Press, 1974) 41.

10. Taylor, *Leaving Church*, 227.

Chapter 8

The Sound of Silence: Remembering Why We're Here

I began this book by having us take a long and painful look at the prophet Elijah languishing under the broom bush, or juniper tree. Weary and fearful, he was ready to toss in his ordination papers. Worse than that, he was ready to die. Life under the juniper tree simply wasn't the kind of life he wanted to keep living.

In the preceding chapters, we have not only looked at Elijah under that juniper tree but also acknowledged that we've spent some frightful time there ourselves. We wanted trumpets in the morning but got loneliness and the juniper tree instead. I've shared what little wisdom I gained in the shadow of that tree and hope that something in this book has given you a measure of hope and encouragement.

As we round the bend now and head toward the finish line, I'd like us to cast our eyes once again at poor Elijah under that tree. After Elijah expressed his suicidal despair, he lay down and slept.

> Then suddenly a messenger tapped him and said to him, "Get up! Eat something!" Elijah opened his eyes and saw flatbread baked on glowing coals and a jar of water right by his head. He ate and drank, and then went back to sleep. The LORD's messenger returned a second time and tapped him. "Get up!" the messenger said. "Eat something because you have a difficult road ahead of you." (1 Kings 19:5-7)

Perhaps the most obvious lesson in that message is that our physical condition always impacts our spiritual condition. More than anything at that moment, Elijah needed flatbread baked on glowing coals and a jar of water. How we ministers eat and sleep is crucial to our ministry. The point of the message seems to be that Elijah couldn't hope to minister effectively if he didn't meet his physical needs. A change in diet, rest, and exercise might well be God's prescription for us, too.

But I'm not sure Elijah wanted to hear the last part of that message, the part about having a difficult road ahead of him. He was under the juniper tree precisely because of the difficult roads he'd already had to navigate. Now he has to walk another one?

But Elijah got up and journeyed to Mount Horeb, God's mountain. The word of the Lord came to him with one question: "Why are you here, Elijah?" (1 Kings 19:9). Elijah replied that he had been passionate for God—that, in fact, he had been the only one in all of Israel willing to take a stand for God. What happens next is one of the most famous scenes in the Old Testament. The Lord says to Elijah, "Go out and stand at the mountain before the LORD. The LORD is passing by" (1 Kings 19:11). A wind roars through the mountain, but God is not in the wind. After the wind, an earthquake shakes the mountain, but God is not in the earthquake. Then a fire blazes through the mountain, but God is not in the fire.

> After the fire, there was a sound. Thin. Quiet. When Elijah heard it, he wrapped his face in his coat. He went out and stood at the cave's entrance. A voice came to him and said, "Why are you here, Elijah?" (1 Kings 19:12-13)

Notice that the only question God wanted the disgruntled prophet to consider was, "Why are you here, Elijah?" Elijah got that question thrown at him not once but twice. I think God posed that question to him because it was the one question he had to answer if he hoped to escape the juniper tree. He had to look again at who he was and what he was supposed to do with the remainder of his life. "Why are you here?" is the one question each of us has to answer when we're discouraged and disillusioned in our ministry.

Why Are You Here?

If we're looking for a silver lining in the cloud that looms over the juniper tree, it is the realization that sitting under that tree forces us to look long and hard at who we are and what we want to do with the rest of our lives. Like it did for Elijah, the juniper tree can prompt us to get up and go to Mount Horeb to ask ourselves, "Why am I here?" Discouragement and disillusionment turn out to be great motivators for introspection.

When we ask ourselves that question, we're talking about the will of God—a topic we Christians talk about all the time. We preach and hear sermons about finding the will of God. We read books on finding the will of God. It would not be stretching the truth, I think, to say that we are often obsessed with the will of God. More than anything we fear that we might miss the will of God for our lives.

What we usually mean when we discuss the will of God is that God has a specific, pre-programmed plan for our lives. We're supposed to marry this particular person, do this particular job, live in this particular house, attend this particular church, and give to this particular ministry. If we can check all the boxes, we can find the will of God and be both happy and useful. If, however, we can't check all the boxes, we've missed the will of God for our lives and are destined for frustration and misery.

But the longer I live and the more I experience life, the more I find myself agreeing with Robert Capon's concept of the will of God that I mentioned in the last chapter. Finding the will of God doesn't mean we stop on the way home to get mouthwash, razor blades, and a pound of chopped chuck; it is God's longing that we take the risk of being nothing but ourselves, desperately in love.

I love that definition of the will of God because it rescues us from the checklist approach that is almost certain to give us spiritual indigestion and acute anxiety. And I love that definition because of the four truths that are embedded in it:

• *God longs for us to be satisfied and joyful.* It is God's will that we discover who we are and do what we are created to do. As Paul puts it so gloriously in Romans 8:31, God is *for* us. Frankly, if God is not for us, let's not waste our time in ministry anyway. Our motivation for ministry is that God not only loves us and is for us, but that God loves everyone and is for everyone. I love the notion of God, the Divine Lover, longing that we discover who we are so that we can joyfully be that person in the world.

• *Life is risky business.* God longs that we will take the risk of being nothing but ourselves. But being nothing but ourselves is risky because not everyone will like who we are. So finding the will of God takes courage, the courage of self-discovery and self-disclosure. Only risk-takers can discover the will of God for their lives.

• *We have to be nothing but ourselves.* It is beyond liberating to realize that we don't have to pretend to be someone we're not. The marathon runner doesn't have to play linebacker. The introvert doesn't have to be the life of the party. And the doubter doesn't have to fake certainty. We get to be ourselves, and, in doing so, affirm all that God has done and continues to do in our lives. Finding the will of God has little to do with checking boxes and everything to do with finding our soul.

• *We are to be desperately in love.* We are to take the risk of being nothing but ourselves, desperately in love. That is the key, I think, to the will of God. All the way through life we are to stay desperately in love. We are to stay in love with God, ourselves, the people around us, the birds and trees and changing seasons, and the absolute miracle of getting to be alive every day. Actually, we're not trying to *find* the will of God, as if it exists out there somewhere if only we can jump through the proper hoops. No, we're simply trying to *experience* the will of God by loving the incredible lives we already have. If we can stay desperately in love, we've found the will of God wherever we happen to live or work or go to church.

I bring up Capon's definition again because I think it is helpful in trying to decide where to turn after the juniper tree. Instead of obsessing over the details of the future, why don't we let Elijah's question—"Why am I here?"—simmer in our hearts? Why don't we quit worrying about the future and get in touch with who we really are and what we really want to do? Why don't we get rid of the burdensome checklist approach to God's will and relax into the truth that God longs for us to be nothing but ourselves, desperately in love?

The View from the Other Side

That was easier said than done when I was a busy pastor. I was so consumed with attending meetings, preparing sermons, and growing a church that I gave precious little thought to experiencing the will of God. After all, I had decided years ago that God had called me to be a pastor, so why bring up the subject of God's will again? I was trying so hard to serve God that I forgot I was supposed to be enjoying God.

That's where the juniper tree comes to our rescue. If we experience enough conflict, misery, and darkness, we are forced to look again at God's will for our lives. The juniper tree proves to be not just a place of depression but also a place of discovery.

Five years ago, I decided to retire as a pastor and see what came next for me. Our church in San Antonio had a big retirement party for me, which was attended by scores of family, friends, and church members. It was a grand celebration—not, I hope, because they were glad to see me go but because they appreciated our thirteen years together.

We stayed in San Antonio for two years after I retired but felt a nudge to move to the Austin area to be closer to our son and daughter and their families. I wanted to focus on writing, too, and to see what I might yet have to say. After a lifetime of speaking words publicly, I was ready for the more indirect approach of writing words privately.

The move to Cedar Park, just out of Austin, has proven to be a wonderful, life-renewing thing for both Sherry and me. It has also afforded me time to ponder thirty-eight years of ministry. Many nights, I still dream of church people, church meetings, and standing in the pulpit to preach. Just last night, I dreamed I was in the pulpit, couldn't find my sermon notes, and couldn't think of one thing to say to the congregation. Five years into retirement, I must still be processing "church stuff" on some subconscious level.

I've had time to think about the joys and heartaches of being a pastor, time to remember with pain the seasons of conflict and with gratitude the seasons of community. Retirement has done for me what the juniper tree used to do—given me opportunity to ponder the will of God for my life and to consider the question, "Why am I here?"

With the fond hope that you can profit from the words of a veteran (old?) minister no longer in the ecclesiastical saddle, I offer you a few final thoughts from the other side. See these, perhaps, as a grab bag of ideas I couldn't find a place for anywhere else in the book. Or if I did find a place for them, know that I think they deserve repeating.

• *Community and conflict are inextricably connected and make church a baffling place.* Once you decide to plug your life into the socket called "church," you get a puzzling mixture of alternating currents. You get the current of community, which is life-enhancing and energizing. You get deep friendships, rich worship experiences, stirring choral music, meaningful ministry opportunities, and the joy of joining hands with fellow believers to help build the kingdom of God. There's nothing much better than being a part of a vibrant community of faith.

But plugging into "church" also plugs you into a painful variety of negatives—bitter conflict, long and boring meetings, debates over trivial issues, doctrinal disputes, ministers with giant egos, and the pressure of having to live within the carefully prescribed boundaries of your church's expectations. The same current that gives you so much joy can also be the source of your greatest frustration. There's nothing much worse than being part of a church that is sucking the very life out of you.

And that is why it is so hard to know if we should stay under the steeple or escape it. Some days, we can't imagine a future without the community. Other days, we can't imagine a future with all the conflict.

• *Ministry is a privilege—wherever it happens.* When I was a pastor, I would have moments when I was filled with gratitude for getting to do what I was doing. Sometimes, in the middle of a sermon, I'd have one of those "for-this-I-was-made" moments that confirmed for me that I was exactly where I needed to be, doing exactly what I needed to do. Those moments were a nice counter-balance to the juniper tree.

Even though I'm retired and not preaching every week, I still have those moments. Last Saturday, I worked in a soup kitchen in downtown Austin and got the same feeling. I was slicing pizza and placing the pieces in cardboard boxes to give to homeless people, and I had one of those "for-this-I was-made" moments. It reminded me that I don't have to be standing behind a pulpit delivering a sermon to be investing in the kingdom; I can also do my part by serving pizza to hungry people.

For the first sixty-two years of my life, I lived under the steeple. Now that I'm no longer in its shadow, I can still find ways to serve, and, I hope, still find ways to be useful to God and people.

• *Church is not for everyone.* As I said, I have lived my whole life in the shadow of the steeple. I started going to Sunday school and church when I was born and continued going to church almost every Sunday for the next sixty-two years. My life, literally, was the church. That's where I got my faith, my friends, and my weekly schedule. The church taught me about God, introduced me to some wonderful people, and transformed my life.

Of course, I knew that not everyone was as "churched" as I was. I had a few friends who never went to church, and I prayed for them often. But, in general, the people I knew were people like me—devout Christians who went to church and believed in God.

Now that I'm retired and no longer have to go to church, I've had the freedom to look around me and see the world with new, "non-churchy" eyes. What I see is that most of the people around me are not involved in church—and, maybe most surprisingly, don't want to be.

I've been forced to see and admit that church is not for everyone. Some people find church stiff and unwelcoming. Some people have been burned by the church and will never return. Some can't believe the church's doctrines. Some think of church people as stern and unforgiving. Some are too introverted to feel comfortable in a place geared only for extroverts. And some have never had church on their radar at all. It's just never been part of their lives and perhaps never will be.

I'm seeing that the church will never reach many people in our culture simply because those people don't want to be reached. It's going to take some kind of grassroots, non-institutional, informal movement to touch many modern people. That means God is going to call some ministers out of the church so that they can serve in unconventional ways. Who better to touch these unchurched folks than unchurched ministers?

• *Disappointment comes from a variety of directions.* Discouragement and disillusionment can come at us from a multitude of directions. Being a minister in the modern world is a lot like a playing a raucous game of dodge ball: you never know where the next projectile is coming from. As I look back now on my years as a pastor, I realize how many balls I tried to dodge and how often I got hit right in the heart.

Disappointment comes because the world is changing so rapidly that we're not equipped to deal with it.

Disappointment comes because fine Christian people—people we thought we knew and trusted—betray and attack us.

Disappointment comes because the church gets mired in trivia and nonessentials and loses its way.

Disappointment comes because we have failed miserably in some areas and wish we had been wiser and more loving.

Disappointment comes, ironically, because we are disappointed and not the sterling examples of joy and abundant life we long to be.

Disappointment comes because the God we have loved and served all our lives is so silent and absent in our deepest hour of need.

With all of those balls coming at us, it's no wonder that some of them strike us squarely in the heart. I now believe that the minister who has never been struck by one of those balls is either unusually blessed—or totally out of touch with reality.

• *Spiritual growth is hard for ministers.* The reason for this is the factor I mentioned earlier: we are trying to reach the general public so we have to be on a spiritual level that communicates with the masses. And, let's be honest, the masses are not especially attuned to spiritual depth. If the masses are on a level 1 wavelength, that's where the church and its ministers have to be, too. Get too deep, and you'll lose your crowd.

That means, unfortunately, that ministers are never encouraged to go deeper, to move beyond level 1 to become "stewards of the mysteries of God," as Paul puts it in 1 Corinthians. Anyone who has to tread water spiritually for too long will grow weary. He or she might even eventually drown. Unless the minister is being challenged, discovering new depths of meaning in the gospel, and experiencing God in new and real ways, the result is all too predictable: weariness or drowning.

Earlier, I quoted a list of statistics that underscored the perilous plight of modern ministers. What we don't know is how many ministers jumped ship because they grew so bored and lifeless in their own spiritual lives that they had nothing new or meaningful to share.

• *The gospel is going to get more and more marginalized.* For all the reasons I mentioned in the first chapter of this book, I think the Christian gospel is not going to be an "easy sell" in our culture. Take the seven factors I named in that chapter, add a few more to them, and what you get is a world not amenable to believing what Christians have always believed.

In our kind of world, the Bible is just one of many holy books, Jesus is just one of many spiritual teachers, the church is just one of many altruistic organizations, and Christianity is just one of many fine religions. To say in our kind of world that we Christians have *the* truth and that our Jesus is *the* way, *the* truth, and *the* life seems both presumptuous and haughty.

While we certainly don't want to be presumptuous and haughty, those of us who minister in the name of Christ also know that if all we're offering the world is one more entrée on the smorgasbord of modern spirituality, we're doomed. If what we're serving is no better than what other religions and organizations are serving, we will have no passion or conviction at all. However presumptuous and haughty we might think the apostle Paul was, we have to envy his zeal. And he got that zeal because he was completely sold out to the way of Jesus.

• *Being an authentic human being trumps being a successful pastor.* I'm not sure I was ever a "successful pastor," as many would define that phrase. I was never pastor of a large church, never invited to preach at conferences and conventions, never achieved anything resembling fame (or fortune!), and never wrote a book that made the *New York Times* bestseller list.

I spent most of my life as the pastor of middle-sized, suburban churches and spent most of my days preparing sermons, visiting hospitals, officiating at weddings and funerals, and attending more committee meetings than I care to remember. What success I had is measured not in statistics but in relationships.

It was my good privilege to be the pastor of the Andice Baptist Church, The Texas Baptist Children's Home, the Heritage Park Baptist Church, and the Woodland Baptist Church and to join hands with the saints in those churches to build the kingdom of God. They certainly blessed me, and I would like to think that I blessed them, too.

But I thought often about those words of my Uncle Glen—that being myself might preclude me being a successful pastor and guarantee that I would become an authentic human being. Now that I no longer have to concern myself with being a successful pastor, that is where I want to focus my attention. I would like to become an authentic human being. I would like to become more joyful, more honest, more sensitive, more the person God created me to be. I would like to think less about growing a church and more about growing my own soul.

A Final Wish

We can be grateful that the picture of Elijah sitting dejectedly under that juniper tree is not the final picture we have of him in the Bible. After his experience on Mount Horeb, he gets up and continues being a prophet. When he had to consider the question, "Why am I here?" he must have decided that the answer was, "I'm here to be a prophet of God." So he goes out and chooses Elisha to be his successor, confronts King Ahab and King Ahaziah about their godless leadership, and then exits the biblical story in spectacular fashion.

Elijah and Elisha make their way to the Jordan River. When they cross the river, Elijah asks Elisha, "What do you want me to do for you before I'm taken away from you?" and Elisha answers, "Let me have twice your spirit" (2 Kings 2:9).

That is a difficult request, Elijah says. But those of us who have seen him sitting under that juniper tree understand Elisha's request completely. Elisha wanted that kind of resiliency and courage for himself. He wanted twice as much tenacity as Elijah had. He wanted to know that if he ever found himself discouraged and disillusioned, then he, too, would have the heart to get up and keep going.

And, as the saga continues, Elisha's wish is granted. After Elijah is mysteriously and miraculously taken up in a whirlwind, Elisha crosses back over the Jordan while being watched at a distance by a group of prophets from Jericho. They observe him and say to one another, "Elijah's spirit has settled on Elisha" (2 Kings 2:15).

That, I suppose, is as good a place as any to end this book. My final wish for you, if you find yourself languishing under the juniper tree, is the same one Elisha had—that you would have double the spirit of Elijah, that Elijah's spirit would settle on you. I wish that you would get up and go to Mount Horeb. I wish that you would consider again why you are here on this earth. And I wish that you would have the courage to continue to be the minister you've been called to be.

Take heart, as I did, in these words from Uncle Glen:

Preach the truth, live it as you understand it and, happily, what you have carried to the people will someday carry you. I promise!

Other available titles from SMYTH&HELWYS

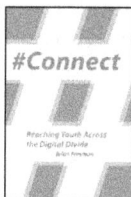

#Connect
Reaching Youth Across the Digital Divide
Brian Foreman

Reaching our youth across the digital divide is a struggle for parents, ministers, and other adults who work with Generation Z—today's teenagers. *#Connect* leads readers into the technological landscape, encourages conversations with teenagers, and reminds us all to be the presence of Christ in every facet of our lives. 978-1-57312-693-9 120 pages/pb **$13.00**

Beginnings
A Reverend and a Rabbi Talk About the Stories of Genesis
Michael Smith and Rami Shapiro

Editor Aaron Herschel Shapiro declares that stories "must be retold—not just repeated, but reinvented, reimagined, and reexperienced" to remain vital in the world. Mike and Rami continue their conversations from the *Mount and Mountain* books, exploring the places where their traditions intersect and diverge, listening to each other as they respond to the stories of Genesis. 978-1-57312-772-1 202 pages/pb **$18.00**

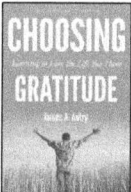

Choosing Gratitude
Learning to Love the Life You Have
James A. Autry

Autry reminds us that gratitude is a choice, a spiritual—not social—process. He suggests that if we cultivate gratitude as a way of being, we may not change the world and its ills, but we can change our response to the world. If we fill our lives with moments of gratitude, we will indeed love the life we have. 978-1-57312-614-4 144 pages/pb **$15.00**

Choosing Gratitude 365 Days a Year
Your Daily Guide to Grateful Living
James A. Autry and Sally J. Pederson

Filled with quotes, poems, and the inspired voices of both Pederson and Autry, in a society consumed by fears of not having "enough"—money, possessions, security, and so on—this book suggests that if we cultivate gratitude as a way of being, we may not change the world and its ills, but we can change our response to the world. 978-1-57312-689-2 210 pages/pb **$18.00**

To order call **1-800-747-3016** or visit **www.helwys.com**

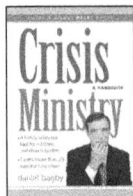

Crisis Ministry: A Handbook
Daniel G. Bagby

Covering more than 25 crisis pastoral care situations, this book provides a brief, practical guide for church leaders and other caregivers responding to stressful situations in the lives of parishioners. It tells how to resource caregiving professionals in the community who can help people in distress.   *978-1-57312-370-9 154 pages/pb* **$15.00**

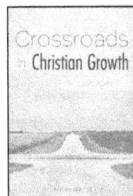

Crossroads in Christian Growth
W. Loyd Allen

Authentic Christian life presents spiritual crises and we struggle to find a hero walking with God at a crossroads. With wisdom and sincerity, W. Loyd Allen presents Jesus as our example and these crises as stages in the journey of growth we each take toward maturity in Christ.   *978-1-57312-753-0 164 pages/pb* **$15.00**

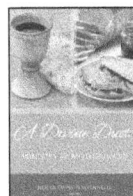

A Divine Duet
Ministry and Motherhood
Alicia Davis Porterfield, ed.

Each essay in this inspiring collection is as different as the mother-minister who wrote it, from theologians to chaplains, inner-city ministers to rural-poverty ministers, youth pastors to preachers, mothers who have adopted, birthed, and done both.   *978-1-57312-676-2 146 pages/pb* **$16.00**

The Exile and Beyond (All the Bible series)
Wayne Ballard

The Exile and Beyond brings to life the sacred literature of Israel and Judah that comprises the exilic and postexilic communities of faith. It covers Ezekiel, Isaiah, Haggai, Zechariah, Malachi, 1 & 2 Chronicles, Ezra, Nehemiah, Joel, Jonah, Song of Songs, Esther, and Daniel.   *978-1-57312-759-2 196 pages/pb* **$16.00**

Fierce Love
Desperate Measures for Desperate Times
Jeanie Miley

Fierce Love is about learning to see yourself and know yourself as a conduit of love, operating from a full heart instead of trying to find someone to whom you can hook up your emotional hose and fill up your empty heart.   *978-1-57312-810-0 276 pages/pb* **$18.00**

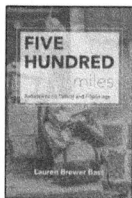

Five Hundred Miles
Reflections on Calling and Pilgrimage
Lauren Brewer Bass

Spain's Camino de Santiago, the Way of St. James, has been a cherished pilgrimage path for centuries, visited by countless people searching for healing, solace, purpose, and hope. These stories from her five-hundred-mile-walk is Lauren Brewer Bass's honest look at the often winding, always surprising journey of a calling. *978-1-57312-812-4 142 pages/pb* **$16.00**

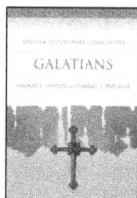

Galatians (Smyth & Helwys Bible Commentary)
Marion L. Soards and Darrell J. Pursiful

In Galatians, Paul endeavored to prevent the Gentile converts from embracing a version of the gospel that insisted on their observance of a form of the Mosaic Law. He saw with a unique clarity that such a message reduced the crucified Christ to being a mere agent of the Law. For Paul, the gospel of Jesus Christ alone, and him crucified, had no place in it for the claim that Law-observance was necessary for believers to experience the power of God's grace. *978-1-57312-771-4 384 pages/hc* **$55.00**

Glimpses from State Street
Wayne Ballard

As a collection of devotionals, *Glimpses from State Street* provides a wealth of insights and new ways to consider and develop our fellowship with Christ. It also serves as a window into the relationship between a small town pastor and a welcoming congregation.

978-1-57312-841-4 158 pages/pb **$15.00**

God's Servants, the Prophets
Bryan Bibb

God's Servants, the Prophets covers the Israelite and Judean prophetic literature from the preexilic period. It includes Amos, Hosea, Isaiah, Micah, Zephaniah, Nahum, Habakkuk, Jeremiah, and Obadiah.

978-1-57312-758-5 208 pages/pb **$16.00**

Gray Matters
100 Devotions for the Aging
Edwin Ray Frazier

"Each line rests on Frazier's fundamental belief that every season in life is valuable and rich with opportunity."

—Alicia Davis Porterfield
Interim pastor and former eldercare chaplain
978-1-57312-837-7 246 pages/pb **$18.00**

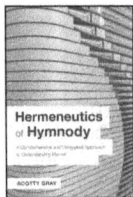

Hermeneutics of Hymnody
A Comprehensive and Integrated Approach to Understanding Hymns
Scotty Gray

Scotty Gray's *Hermeneutics of Hymnody* is a comprehensive and integrated approach to understanding hymns. It is unique in its holistic and interrelated exploration of seven of the broad facets of this most basic forms of Christian literature. A chapter is devoted to each and relates that facet to all of the others. *978-157312-767-7 432 pages/pb* **$28.00**

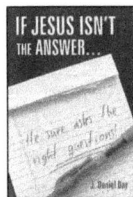

If Jesus Isn't the Answer . . . He Sure Asks the Right Questions!
J. Daniel Day

Taking eleven of Jesus' questions as its core, Day invites readers into their own conversation with Jesus. Equal parts testimony, theological instruction, pastoral counseling, and autobiography, the book is ultimately an invitation to honest Christian discipleship. *978-1-57312-797-4 148 pages/pb* **$16.00**

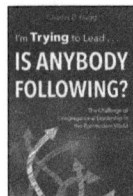

I'm Trying to Lead . . . Is Anybody Following?
The Challenge of Congregational Leadership in the Postmodern World
Charles B. Bugg

Bugg provides us with a view of leadership that has theological integrity, honors the diversity of church members, and reinforces the brave hearts of church leaders who offer vision and take risks in the service of Christ and the church. *978-1-57312-731-8 136 pages/pb* **$13.00**

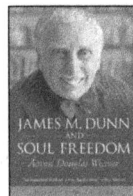

James M. Dunn and Soul Freedom
Aaron Douglas Weaver

James Milton Dunn, over the last fifty years, has been the most aggressive Baptist proponent for religious liberty in the US. Soul freedom—voluntary, uncoerced faith and an unfettered individual conscience before God—is the basis of his understanding of church-state separation and the historic Baptist basis of religious liberty. *978-1-57312-590-1 224 pages/pb* **$18.00**

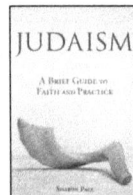

Judaism
A Brief Guide to Faith and Practice
Sharon Pace

Sharon Pace's newest book is a sensitive and comprehensive introduction to Judaism. How does belief in the One God and a universal morality shape the way in which Jews see the world? How does one find meaning in life and the courage to endure suffering? How does one mark joy and forge community ties? *978-1-57312-644-1 144 pages/pb* **$16.00**

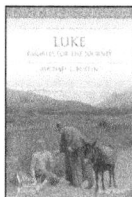

Luke (Smyth & Helwys Annual Bible Study series)
Parables for the Journey
Michael L. Ruffin

These stories in Luke's Gospel are pilgrimage parables. They are parables for those on the way to being the people of God. They are not places where we stop and stay; they are rather places where we learn what we need to learn and from which, equipped with Jesus' directions, we continue the journey. But we will see that they are also places to which we repeatedly return.

Teaching Guide 978-1-57312-849-0 146 pages/pb **$14.00**

Study Guide 978-1-57312-850-6 108 pages/pb **$6.00**

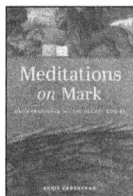

Meditations on Mark
Daily Devotions from the Oldest Gospel
Chris Cadenhead

Readers searching for a fresh encounter with Scripture can delve into *Meditations on Mark*, a collection of daily devotions intended to guide the reader through the book of Mark, the Oldest Gospel and the first known effort to summarize and proclaim the life and ministry of Jesus.

978-1-57312-851-3 158 pages/pb **$15.00**

Meeting Jesus Today
For the Cautious, the Curious, and the Committed
Jeanie Miley

Meeting Jesus Today, ideal for both individual study and small groups, is intended to be used as a workbook. It is designed to move readers from studying the Scriptures and ideas within the chapters to recording their journey with the Living Christ.

978-1-57312-677-9 320 pages/pb **$19.00**

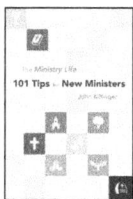

The Ministry Life
101 Tips for New Ministers
John Killinger

Sharing years of wisdom from more than fifty years in ministry and teaching, *The Ministry Life: 101 Tips for New Ministers* by John Killinger is filled with practical advice and wisdom for a minister's day-to-day tasks as well as advice on intellectual and spiritual habits to keep ministers of any age healthy and fulfilled.

978-1-57312-662-5 244 pages/pb **$19.00**

To order call **1-800-747-3016** or visit **www.helwys.com**

Mount and Mountain
Vol. 2: A Reverend and a Rabbi Talk About the Sermon on the Mount
Rami Shapiro and Michael Smith

This book, focused on the Sermon on the Mount, represents the second half of Mike and Rami's dialogue. In it, Mike and Rami explore the text of Jesus' sermon cooperatively, contributing perspectives drawn from their lives and religious traditions and seeking moments of illumination. *978-1-57312-654-0 254 pages/pb* **$19.00**

Of Mice and Ministers
Musings and Conversations About Life, Death, Grace, and Everything
Bert Montgomery

With stories about pains, joys, and everyday life, *Of Mice and Ministers* finds Jesus in some unlikely places and challenges us to do the same. From tattooed women ministers to saying the "N"-word to the brotherly kiss, Bert Montgomery takes seriously the lesson from Psalm 139— where can one go that God is not already there? *978-1-57312-733-2 154 pages/pb* **$14.00**

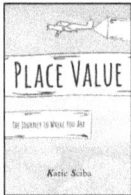

Place Value
The Journey to Where You Are
Katie Sciba

Does a place have value? Can a place change us? Is it possible for God to use the place you are in to form you? From Victoria, Texas to Indonesia, Belize, Australia, and beyond, Katie Sciba's wanderlust serves as a framework to understand your own places of deep emotion and how God may have been weaving redemption around you all along.
978-157312-829-2 138 pages/pb **$15.00**

Reading Joshua
(Reading the Old Testament series)
A Historical-Critical/Archaeological Commentary
John C. H. Laughlin

Using the best of current historical-critical studies by mainstream biblical scholars, and the most recent archaeological discoveries and theorizing, Laughlin questions both the historicity of the stories presented in the book as well as the basic theological ideology presented through these stories: namely that Yahweh ordered the indiscriminate butchery of the Canaanites.
978-1-57312-836-0 274 pages/pb **$32.00**

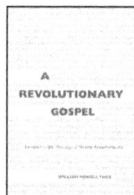

A Revolutionary Gospel
Salvation in the Theology of Walter Rauschenbusch
William Powell Tuck

William Powell Tuck describes how Rauschenbusch's concept of redemption requires a transformation of society as well as individuals—and that no one can genuinely be redeemed without this redemption affecting the social culture as well. *A Revolutionary Gospel* shows us how Rauschenbusch's revolutionary concept of salvation is still relevant today.

978-1-57312-804-9 190 pages/pb **$21.00**

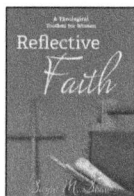

Reflective Faith
A Theological Toolbox for Women
Susan M. Shaw

In *Reflective Faith*, Susan Shaw offers a set of tools to explore difficult issues of biblical interpretation, theology, church history, and ethics—especially as they relate to women. Reflective faith invites intellectual struggle and embraces the unknown; it is a way of discipleship, a way to love God with your mind, as well as your heart, your soul, and your strength.

978-1-57312-719-6 292 pages/pb **$24.00**

Workbook *978-1-57312-754-7 164 pages/pb* **$12.00**

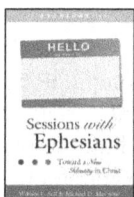

Sessions with Ephesians
(Sessions Bible Studies series)
Toward a New Identity in Christ
William L. Self & Michael D. McCullar

Ephesians has been called "the most contemporary book in the Bible." Strip it of just a few first-century references and it would be easily applicable to the modern church.

978-1-57312-838-4 110 pages/pb **$14.00**

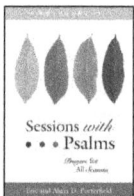

Sessions with Psalms (Sessions Bible Studies series)
Prayers for All Seasons
Eric and Alicia D. Porterfield

Useful to seminar leaders during preparation and group discussion, as well as in individual Bible study, *Sessions with Psalms* is a ten-session study designed to explore what it looks like for the words of the psalms to become the words of our prayers. Each session is followed by a thought-provoking page of questions.

978-1-57312-768-4 136 pages/pb **$14.00**

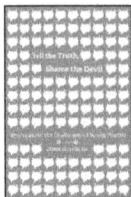

Tell the Truth, Shame the Devil
Stories about the Challenges of Young Pastors
James Elllis III, ed.

A pastor's life is uniquely difficult. *Tell the Truth, Shame the Devil*, then, is an attempt to expose some of the challenges that young clergy often face. While not exhaustive, this collection of essays is a superbly compelling and diverse introduction to how tough being a pastor under the age of thirty-five can be. 978-1-57312-839-1 *198 pages/pb* **$18.00**

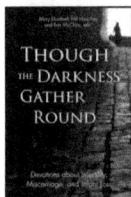

Though the Darkness Gather Round
Devotions about Infertility, Miscarriage, and Infant Loss
Mary Elizabeth Hill Hanchey and Erin McClain, eds.

Much courage is required to weather the long grief of infertility and the sudden grief of miscarriage and infant loss. This collection of devotions by men and women, ministers, chaplains, and lay leaders who can speak of such sorrow, is a much-needed resource and precious gift for families on this journey and the faith communities that walk beside them.

978-1-57312-811-7 *180 pages/pb* **$19.00**

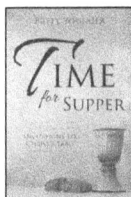

Time for Supper
Invitations to Christ's Table
Brett Younger

Some scholars suggest that every meal in literature is a communion scene. Could every meal in the Bible be a communion text? Could every passage be an invitation to God's grace? These meditations on the Lord's Supper help us listen to the myriad of ways God invites us to gratefully, reverently, and joyfully share the cup of Christ. 978-1-57312-720-2 *246 pages/pb* **$18.00**

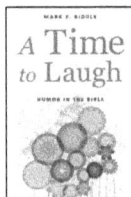

A Time to Laugh
Humor in the Bible
Mark E. Biddle

With characteristic liveliness, Mark E. Biddle explores the ways humor was intentionally incorporated into Scripture. Drawing on Biddle's command of Hebrew language and cultural subtleties, *A Time to Laugh* guides the reader through the stories of six biblical characters who did rather unexpected things. 978-1-57312-683-0 *164 pages/pb* **$14.00**

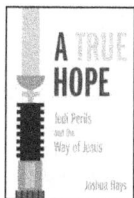

A True Hope
Jedi Perils and the Way of Jesus
Joshua Hays

Star Wars offers an accessible starting point for considering substantive issues of faith, philosophy, and ethics. In *A True Hope*, Joshua Hays explores some of these challenging ideas through the sayings of the Jedi Masters, examining the ways the worldview of the Jedi is at odds with that of the Bible. *978-1-57312-770-7 186 pages/pb* **$18.00**

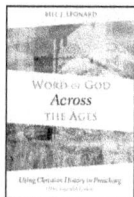

Word of God Across the Ages
Using Christian History in Preaching
Bill J. Leonard

In this third, enlarged edition, Bill J. Leonard returns to the roots of the Christian story to find in the lives of our faithful forebears examples of the potent presence of the gospel. Through these stories, those who preach today will be challenged and inspired as they pursue the divine Word in human history through the ages. *978-1-57312-828-5 174 pages/pb* **$19.00**

The World Is Waiting for You
Celebrating the 50th Ordination Anniversary of Addie Davis
Pamela R. Durso & LeAnn Gunter Johns, eds.

Hope for the church and the world is alive and well in the words of these gifted women. Keen insight, delightful observations, profound courage, and a gift for communicating the good news are woven throughout these sermons. The Spirit so evident in Addie's calling clearly continues in her legacy. *978-1-57312-732-5 224 pages/pb* **$18.00**

With Us in the Wilderness
Finding God's Story in Our Lives
Laura A. Barclay

What stories compose your spiritual biography? In *With Us in the Wilderness*, Laura Barclay shares her own stories of the intersection of the divine and the everyday, guiding readers toward identifying and embracing God's presence in their own narratives.

978-1-57312-721-9 120 pages/pb **$13.00**

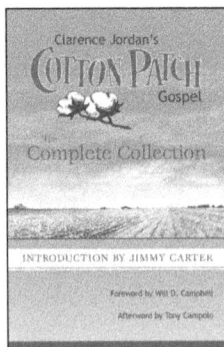

www.ingramcontent.com/pod-product-compliance
Lightning Source LLC
Chambersburg PA
CBHW071349090426
42738CB00012B/3065